The DECOUPAGE ·KIT·

The
DECOUPAGE
·KIT·

Creative ideas • Simple techniques • Beautiful projects

Belinda Ballantine

Photography by Sue Atkinson

Little, Brown and Company
Boston • New York • Toronto • London

In memory of my talented parents, Sheila and Neil.

A LITTLE, BROWN BOOK

This edition first published in 1993
Second printing 1993

ISBN 0-316-90598-4

A CIP catalogue record for this book is available from the British Library.

AN EDDISON·SADD EDITION
Edited, designed and produced by
Eddison Sadd Editions Limited
St Chad's Court
146B King's Cross Road
London WC1X 9DH

Phototypeset in ITC Modern No. 216 by
Dorchester Typesetting Group, Dorset, England.
Colour originated Columbia Offset, Hong Kong.
Produced by Mandarin Offset, printed and bound in Hong Kong.

Little, Brown and Company (UK) Ltd
Brettenham House, Lancaster Place
London WC2E 7EN

CONTENTS

INTRODUCTION

DISCOVERING DECOUPAGE

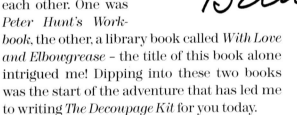

Having always been a great believer in fate, it was not in the least bit surprising to me that in 1974 I was lent two books, both on the subject of painted furniture, within a week of each other. One was *Peter Hunt's Workbook*, the other, a library book called *With Love and Elbowgrease* – the title of this book alone intrigued me! Dipping into these two books was the start of the adventure that has led me to writing *The Decoupage Kit* for you today.

I had always loved painted furniture; but this was before its current rise in popularity, so friends thought I was a little mad when I took my first hesitant steps into the world of brush-strokes. Having devoured and doodled from all the books on folk-art in the local library, designs and shapes flooded my mind and I would wake each morning to the thrill of another whole day of experimenting with a paintbrush.

Junk shops and auction sales became Aladdin's caves; and I lived with the conviction that the next acquisition would be the best ever. My little car, laden with ghastly-brown damaged bits and pieces, would proudly wend its way home as if it was full of treasure.

In those days, 'distressing' and other paint 'finishes' had not been developed, so each piece was lovingly mended and prepared: filled, primed, an undercoat painted and a glowing new coat of gloss or oil-based eggshell paint given in bright emerald, red or deep blue, on my kitchen table. They were then left to dry, and while doing so, each one seemed to tell me how it would like to look, whether it would like to be covered in roses and leaves or twining ribbons. The ideas and themes for all the designs being drawn from earlier doodles.

These were exciting, happy days for me, and cheerful, if somewhat amateur, pieces of furniture emerged. I began painting things for my two small daughters' rooms, then aged two and four, which pleased them immensely, so they quickly learnt not to touch the wet paint. I suspect they had more 'rests' and 'naps' than most small children, and were always in bed on time so that I could paint for a few hours in the evening!

For 18 months I painted furniture for one shop; there were no restrictions on what I painted as long as the finished piece blended with stripped pine. I derived so much pleasure from my newly-discovered talent that it felt as though I had been given the most wonderful present all of a sudden. In return I determined that one day I would share that joy by showing others how to get as much satisfaction from painting as I did and still do.

I spent ten years trying to improve the dreaded brush-stroke (which appears to be very easy, but in fact involves an unfamiliar and quite complicated hand action), learning by trial and error what worked and what did not. Then one day I was privileged enough to be asked to teach furniture painting at an interior design school in London, England for a day. That first lesson was terrifying. I had no idea how to teach and was extremely nervous; those poor students who attended my first class may well have been put off painting for life!

Determination prevailed and gradually I evolved a way of teaching design work that was manageable for most people, but there were still a few who found the freehand brush-stroke almost impossible – so frustrating for them when the urge to be creative was so great. I began to wonder how I could help these enthusiastic students to achieve their aims in spite of their difficulties.

A few years later, I had the great pleasure of learning to gild in London, England with Vonda and Jack Jessup of the Academy of Decorative Finishes, Arizona, US. This opened up a new dimension in decoration for me, so a year later I returned for more inspiration at their hands. Imagine my horror when halfway through the week-long course we were presented with an incredibly intricate black and white photocopy of a cartouche frame and a pair of scissors with tiny blades, then asked to cut it out for use in a decoupage project. My fellow students started snipping and most were finished within the hour. I was only a quarter of the way round and had amputated various cherubs' appendages, pruned foliage and my scissor finger and thumb were in agony. This was definitely not for me!

A few months later, having discovered the wonders of Dover publications, a vast array of copyright-free picture source-books that appeal to all tastes, fortunately I tried cutting out motifs again. After a while my fingers became more nimble and did not ache so much, and I began to get huge satisfaction from the growing pile of neat cut-outs.

At that time I had several commissions for hand-painted clock-faces, which take a surprisingly long time to paint. One day my younger daughter, who was by then 18 and ever practical, suggested that I should paint one really good clock-face and then have it colour photocopied. What a great idea! It set me thinking about all the people who found the freehand brush-stroke so difficult. Why not paint the designs they liked myself and have them colour copied; then students could cut out the designs and stick them, so that when finished, a project would still look hand-painted.

The coral roses and bows used on the step-by-step clock-face (*see pages 76-7*) was the first design produced in this way. Once again I felt the initial thrill of planning and painting pretty designs, but this time with the added pleasure of knowing that anyone could use them, in any way they liked, to satisfy their own creative urges, using a colour of their choice for the background.

So, this is the roundabout way I discovered the joy of decoupage. Still not knowing very much about the specific techniques involved, back I went to the Dover Bookshop to acquire Hiram Manning's book, *Manning on Decoupage*. The photographs of furniture and boxes in it were wonderful, but on starting to read, I discovered to my horror that it was imperative to finish an object with 30–100 coats of varnish. Being a creature of instant gratification, with a very low boredom threshold, this very nearly deterred me from my resolve again! Did all decoupage really have to have that many coats of varnish and did it always have to be oil-based? At a coat a day, to allow for drying time, it would take at least a month just to varnish a piece! I decided the only way to find out if so many coats of varnish were really vital was to experiment.

Since Manning's book was written, many more durable and reliable water-based products have appeared on the market, so I set about seeing if they, or a combination of them and oil-based products, would form an adequate protective layer, and to my delight they did! I also tried various other lacquers and varnishes to see which combinations of products would work and in which order. Discovering the longevity of any of these combinations will have to be for the future as none of the pieces are more than two years old at present. But having convinced myself that it need not take a month to finish a project, I set about decoupage in earnest.

As with the painted furniture, my main interest in decoupage lies in designing: balancing shape with space, colour with colour and adapting a design to fit any shaped facet. So, although I will never be as perfectionistic as Mr Manning, I hope that the use of all sorts of paper from plain white paper to my painted designs will be a source of inspiration to you, allowing your imagination to adapt and expand my ideas to suit your own taste.

So many things in our lives influence our taste. When people talk of 'good taste', what they really mean is that *they* like it, so never feel nervous of doing something if it pleases you. Furthermore, never be frightened of experimenting. I have learnt far more from my disasters than I ever did from the successes! Amazing new 'finishes' are often discovered as you watch something go badly wrong, with the paint peeling or curdling. Far better for that to happen on an experiment than on the special gift that has to be finished and ready that very day.

The more I learn, the more I realize how much more there is to discover. Why chain oneself to only tried and tested methods and designs, repeating simply what has gone before? I love Victorian 'scraps' and black and white prints, but also tissue-paper, sandpaper and doilies, and I love painting designs, which I hope will give others pleasure. Before you dive into your first decoupage project, however, you might like to know a little about the history of decoupage.

THE ORIGINS OF DECOUPAGE

The word, 'decoupage' is derived from the French word *découpure* which simply means 'cutting out'. A piece of decoupage was created by Marie Antoinette as early as *c.* 1780. Written on it were the words: '*Découpure faite par la Reine*'. Decoupage today means using paper cut-outs to enhance furnishings and accessories. The art is a simple one, you merely select the illustrations, cut them out, arrange them in any design, stick them down and varnish over them.

Long before decoupage, as we know it today, became an art form, paper cutting itself, without the involvement of varnish, was used in decoration. Paper, or vellum, was a readily available material, and even in medieval times and probably earlier, cut-outs were used to decorate the edges of manuscripts; and stencils, also a form of paper cutting, were used as a guide for embellishing walls with a design hundreds of years ago.

Ever since the wall-paintings of prehistory, there has been an urge to beautify our surroundings with decoration: painting and drawing being the main form of visual expression; in each era and situation people used whatever materials were available at the time. For centuries there seems to have been a desire to re-create or imitate substances and textures if the real thing was not available, or was too expensive; finding a way to fake it or faux (a much nicer word). Marble, for instance, was re-created with paint and glaze, *trompe-l'œil* grisailles used to imitate carving and decoupage to imitate Chinese lacquerwork.

If we go back to the middle of the seventeenth century in Britain, before decoupage, as we now know it, had a name, we will find that after the dreary and restrictive years of the English Civil War, the Restoration came as a breath of fresh air. Re-awakening of all kinds of creativity: writing, fashion and interior design all took a gleeful leap forward, encouraged by a thirst for beauty and elegance in all things.

At that time, paper cutting itself was an art-form, techniques often involved the use of glue, but not varnish. The dexterous handling of a pair of scissors or penknife was encouraged in the education of young noble-ladies throughout Europe, alongside painting, embroidery and music, so those skills already existed long before the advent of decoupage.

Fine quilling was used to create pictures and dress wax figurines, cutting thin strips of coloured and gold paper, winding them tightly round a quill to form a coil that was then shaped and stuck to the surface in imitation of raised embellishments, such as embossing, filigree or embroidery.

Portraits of famous people were intricately cut from white paper, all the little shadows of the face, like the shading lines on a print, were parallel slivers of paper, cut away with total accuracy, then the finished piece was mounted on black paper to show the contrast. Birds and amazingly fine baskets of flowers were cut in this way too, often each of the birds' feathers was cut in every detail and applied individually, and the flowers so fine that they resembled lace.

Another fashionable art-form was the cutting of silhouettes; this time from black paper mounted on white.

Gazing at these unbelievably complex feats of cutting makes you realize how easy it was for those exponents to adapt to the decoupage that was to come.

Ever since the thirteenth century when Marco Polo brought back tales of wonder from his travels, there had been an interest in China, but trade during the next few centuries was mainly devoted to spices, silk and eventually their beautiful porcelain. It was not until the Reformation when Charles II renewed the East India Company's charter that lacquerwork began to be imported into the West.

Lacquer had been discovered during the Han dynasty over 1,800 years earlier and was made from the sap of the sumac plant. In 1680, the reigning emperor, K'ang Hsi, established a royal lacquerwork factory next to the palace in Peking and boxes and furniture from there began to arrive in Europe.

The sheer beauty and refreshing difference of the technique took the West by storm, so different was it to anything that had been seen before. Lacquer, or varnish, was unknown in the West up until the seventeenth century, polished oak had reigned supreme until then. The exuberance of the lacquerwork furniture created a passion for it all over a Europe thirsting for novelty in the new age of elegance. Royal and noble patrons had an insatiable desire for it, anyone who was anyone had to have some, but there was not

enough lacquerware available to meet the demand.

From the time in 1682 when Louis XIV received two pieces of red lacquerware from the Siamese royal family, his and every court in Europe from Sweden to Russia had to have a Chinese pavilion.

Since the demand for lacquerware was greater than the supply, enterprising business people knew well that there would be a market for replicas. So it was not long before craftsmen in cabinet-making across Europe determined to find a way of imitating the effect of Chinese lacquerwork.

In Italy, 'Lacca contrafatta' was produced; using coloured-paper prints of Chinese paintings over prepared background, followed by layers of lacquer or varnish. These resembled their source of inspiration so beautifully that the idea of using paper cut-outs to imitate lacquerware quickly spread across Europe. In France, the Martin brothers opened three factories of 'Vernis Martin' furniture.

In England the technique was called 'Japanning' (probably because by the sixteenth century the Japanese, who had received the recipe from Korean invaders in the sixth century, were even better at it than the Chinese), and in 1688 John Stalker and George Parker published their *Treatise of Japanning and Varnishing*. This included detailed instructions on how to create the desired finish, or in other words how to apply varnish.

Everyone jumped on the 'lust for lacquerware' bandwagon; French artists such as Jean Pillement and Boucher produced Chinese-style prints specially designed for cutting out and sticking, published in London in 1757. I say 'Chinese-style' because very few people had actually been to China in those days, only those privileged enough to hold trading concessions at specific ports were allowed to land and then only for the short time needed to trade. So all the designs were produced from what artists had seen of lacquerware and porcelain, combined with their, sometimes vivid, imaginations!

It is hard to appreciate in today's world, where we are lucky if a fashion or trend lasts more than ten years, how that early Chinese

lacquerwork created a passion for all forms of chinoiserie that lasted for over 100 years. Think of Chinese Chippendale, the Prince Regent's Pavilion in Brighton and the faux bamboo of the early nineteenth century; so its popularity not only heralded the advent of decoupage, but has influenced style ever since.

In 1762 Robert Sayer published *The Ladies Amusement, or the whole Art of Japanning made easy*, which included over 1,500 hand-coloured designs for his readers to cut out: 'For joining in groups or to be placed singly'. They were to be neatly cut with scissors, or the sharp point of a knife, brushed on the back with gum water, or thin paste (no mention of sealing the prints first!), and stuck down. For Japanning, seven coats of 'seedlac' applied over the top, or 12 for preference, were recommended. Could this be the first mention of my beloved, shellac, a type of honey-coloured lacquer?

By the eighteenth century decoupage had been taken up by Royalty, nobility and gentry all over Europe and America. And in 1772 Mrs Mary Delany embarked on a new interpretation of the craft. Since childhood she had been skilled in the use of scissors, as well as being an accomplished embroideress and talented artist; amongst her friends were some of the greatest botanists of that time, who brought thousands of new plants back to this country from all over the world. She fell upon the idea of reproducing plants to scale, not by painting them, but by cutting each stalk, leaf, petal and stamen from appropriately coloured pieces of paper. Each shadow or highlight was separately cut and all were stuck, layer upon layer to a black background, giving the plants and flowers an almost three-dimensional look. Her Bay-leaved passion flower, *Passiflora laurifolia*, has over 230 minute, separately- and accu-rately-cut petals from about four shades of paper, glued with unbelievable accuracy.

During the next ten years she made over 1,000 of these flower collages, or as she jokingly called them, her 'Flora Delanica'. The most amazing part of all is that she was born in 1700, so did not start this astounding feat, now housed in the British museum, until she was 72! And ended it only because of failing eyesight when she was 82.

Inevitably, the vogue for Eastern exotica could not go on forever; by about 1830, Victorian romanticism took over. After a short lull in popularity decoupage changed totally to become almost unrecognizable from its eighteenth-century origins. The art of paper cutting waned as multi-coloured embossed 'scraps' began to be produced in Germany, America and England. The subjects were very different from the original Chinese-style ones. Children, pets, storybook characters, costume fashions and pretty flowers galore: since they were half cut out already, little skill was needed to improve them and usually they were used as they were. The style altered; they were placed pell-mell, overlapping randomly, usually around a larger print that acted as a central motif. Such things as 'scrap screens' as advocated by *Cassell's Household Guide* of 1875 became popular.

Since Victorian times, decoupage has sadly fallen into neglect, apart from a small number of ardent devotees. Its most recent resurgence is not only overdue, but heartily welcomed.

With today's technology opening up so many new possibilities for decoupage as an enjoyable pastime as well as a veritable art form, creating pleasure and beauty for ourselves and others for very little expense, this is the perfect time to re-explore decoupage for all manner of decorative purposes.

LEFT. A selection of decoupage projects using a variety of different paper, some with wrapping paper and some with black and white photocopies. A box specially for Christmas features one of my designs of holly wreath and tartan ribbons, and the frame is decoupaged with music singed at the edges and antiqued.

PART ONE

TECHNIQUES

This section of the book gives you detailed instructions on the techniques used for all the projects demonstrated in the second part of this book. Not only does it give you step-by-step accounts of how to choose, cut, arrange, stick and varnish paper cut-outs, but it also shows you how to achieve a multitude of other decorative effects, such as eye-catching paint finishes, gilding and crackle varnishing, to add the finishing touches to your decoupage items. All specialist equipment, materials and their US equivalents are described fully in the glossary on page 125.

Source Materials

The possibilities for decoration with decoupage are endless. Almost any pliable material can be used: from glossy colour magazines to maps; old catalogues to fabric; sheet music to botanical prints; wrapping paper to wallpaper – the list is endless. And with this kit, hand-painted sheets of motifs created especially for decoupage are provided for you to colour photocopy and use.

BELOW. *Two variations for decoupaging with Victorian scraps, widely available from museums and craft shops. On the clockface, individual flowers cut and arranged; on the can, scraps overlap solidly from the child's face outwards.*

MAGAZINES

Provided they are printed on a good quality paper, magazines can yield all sorts of inspiration: advertisements for lavish jewellery, country pursuit magazines full of birds and animals, gardening catalogues full of sumptuous flowers, travel brochures with mouth-watering sunsets. Whole pages can be used as a background, decoupaging on top like collage, or single motifs can be cut. Always test magazine paper with a coat of sealer or water-based varnish before cutting, to see if the reverse side shows through.

WRAPPING PAPER

The wrapping papers available today offer a vast selection of styles, colours and tastes; they provide scope for countless wonderful projects from children's furniture, using cartoon images, to screens and headboards cascading with shrub roses. With plain coloured papers you can add striking borders to enhance any design, alternatively you can simply cut around templates. Simple white writing-paper can look very effective and gold or silver can add a touch of splendour.

VICTORIAN 'SCRAPS'

Reproductions of old-fashioned 'scraps' are now widely available from craft shops, museums and mail order. These can be cut out and used either overlapping one another so that almost the entire surface is covered, the technique favoured by Victorian decoupers, or, alternatively the motifs can be cut into smaller segments and arranged in an attractive design (*see bottom left*).

PRINTS

Traditionally, paper designs used for decoupage have been influenced by the beautiful examples from the seventeenth and eighteenth centuries. Many of these are reproduced now in the numerous copyright-free books available today. These designs can be photocopied and used over and over again without destroying the original book; they can be enlarged or reduced to fit any size project, even if the enlargement stretches over several sheets of paper, it can be

RIGHT. *Here is a wondrous array of source materials, such as wrapping paper, white and gold doilies, pictures from magazines, various black and white prints and a selection of Belinda's own hand-painted designs.*

judiciously cut and joined together to look like one large piece. Usually photocopies appear a little darker than the original, but it is possible to adjust them at the touch of a button.

HAND-TINTED PRINTS

In the eighteenth century, when decoupage became popular as a substitute for lacquerware, black and white prints were often tinted in soft colours, before cutting out, to imitate their source of inspiration. Then, paints were made mostly from powder pigments, nowadays we can use either pencil crayons, watercolours or artists' acrylics to achieve the same effect. Before using for decoupage, hand-tinted prints must be sealed, the type of sealer used and whether you seal before or after tinting depend on which tinting medium you employ. Watercolour paint must be sealed with a spirit-based lacquer, such as sanding sealer because water-based varnish would make the colour run. Acrylic tube paints and pencil crayons, however, are waterproof and therefore ideal for use with water-based varnish, sanding sealer or shellac, to age them. With them you also have the choice of sealing the print before or after tinting it; sealing first makes it less absorbent and easier to give an even wash, also to wipe off any small mistakes. Sealing them after tinting is just as effective.

Whichever paint you choose, a very thin wash must be mixed on a plate, diluting the paint with plenty of water. Tint the design

with your chosen colour using a large brush, and allow to dry. Then mix a slightly stronger version of the same colour to paint in the shaded areas, and a stronger one again for the darkest shaded areas. Try to use another colour to darken your tones, rather than reaching for the black: a little red to darken greens, and brown to darken blues or yellows.

COLOUR PHOTOCOPIES

Modern technology has given us the wonderful colour copier, which is capable of amazing feats! Black and white prints can be reproduced in any shade, and similarly you can reproduce a multi-coloured image in a single colour or in the negative of its colours; pictures or photographs can be enlarged by 400 per cent (eight times their original size), or reduced by 50 per cent (a quarter of their original size); they can be stretched in either direction, to turn a circle into an oval and vice versa; or reversed to give the mirror image. It is even possible on the more advanced colour copiers to give a picture the texture of tapestry, and using the 'magic pen' you can select areas of the picture to be printed repeatedly all over the sheet. Any flat coloured surface can be copied, fabric for example. It is useful to remember that colour copiers tend to print a little brighter than the original, but that can be adjusted using the controls.

RIGHT. *Here are three examples of more unusual materials that can be used for decoupage. Animal motifs cut from sandpaper for the red box, sections of gold doilies for the blue box and geometric shapes cut from plain white and marbled papers for the black octagonal box.*

OTHER MATERIALS

There are an infinite number of sources to draw from, just let your imagination roam. Doilies, plain white or metallic gold, are a cheap and versatile material to decoupage with. Their textured surface gives a marvellous embossed effect when given an antique look with Raw Umber emulsion (*see page 39 and glossary*). For a textured look, simple shapes cut out of coarse sandpaper also make effective motifs, especially if applied to a painted surface and then gilded. One-sided metallic paper or marbled paper, cut into strips with a ruler and craft knife, are useful for borders. Old sheet music, wallpaper, maps, even comics all make excellent materials for decoupage. If you wish to use photographs it is best to use colour photocopies of them.

SEALING PRINTS

Paper has a tendency to stretch when covered with water-based adhesives; the thinner the paper and the larger the cut-out, the more it will distort and stretch, causing wrinkles and air bubbles. If the paper has been sealed first this can be avoided.

There are various suitable products: water-based varnish, or one of the shellac family are best. I prefer sanding sealer or 'white polish', a bleached, almost colourless version of the brown shellac. It gives the paper a brittle feel, making it easier to cut; it also takes the brightness out of new white photocopies. For a deeper parchment colour, mix sanding sealer with a little brown shellac.

Water-based varnish is equally as effective, its advantage being that it is totally colourless and merely leaves the paper with a plastic feel. Alternatively, waterproof PVA glue (*see glossary*) diluted with water to a thin spreadable consistency can be used. Thinner types of wallpaper paste can also be used.

Whichever you choose, it should be applied to both sides of the print and allowed to dry before cutting out, this makes the cut-out waterproof and more durable.

THICKENING AND THINNING PRINTS

Some materials need special treatment to thicken or thin the paper before it can be used. To thicken thin paper, you can coat it with sanding sealer or water-based varnish. Very flimsy paper, such as tissue-paper, cannot be successfully thickened, instead we use a different method of sticking (*see page 119*). Thicker materials, on the other hand, cards or postcards for example, may need thinning to make them easier to work with. The best way to reduce thickness is to paint the wrong side with a thick sealer, such as shellac, or PVA glue, and when dry, ease between the layers at one corner. Remove the backing paper by placing a pencil across one corner and rolling the paper around it, until a layer has been removed. I have not found this an ideal method, as the remaining layer of paper is usually uneven.

TRANSFERS

Rather than risk tearing or ruining the print by trying to thin it, you may find it easier to make a transfer, or 'decal', from it. This is not strictly decoupage as it does not involve cutting around motifs, however, it does eliminate the raised paper edges. Therefore it is very useful when you are short of time for varnishing. If, however, you wish to use transfers to decoupage a large object, they must be made in sections and arranged. This, obviously, eradicates the advantage of an instantly smooth surface, necessitating more coats of varnish, but it does allow the use of prints that may otherwise be difficult to work with. These transfers are excellent for items that need to be very durable, such as table-mats, or for designs that are too intricate to cut out. It is possible to make transfers from coloured prints, but results vary depending on the surface of the print.

To make a transfer, begin by sticking the print to a non-porous board with masking tape, then brush on layers of decalling fluid (*see glossary*). Step-by-step instructions for the rest of the procedure are shown overleaf.

MAKING TRANSFERS

1 Apply six–eight coats of decalling fluid in alternate directions, vertically and horizontally, drying between coats. Detach print and masking tape together when final coat is dry and submerge in warm water.

2 Remove from water after 1–2 hours. Using tips of fingers gently rub paper off back of soggy print, leaving ink in the plastic film remaining. This will gradually become transparent when applied to the object.

FINISHING

Once attached to the object press the transfer firmly all over using a slightly damp sponge to eliminate any possible air bubbles that are trapped beneath the surface. Take care not to press too hard as the transfer is still stretchy and wrinkles can occur. This stretchiness is very useful for borders encircling the outside of an object, especially box lids where the top design overlaps the edges. Trim the transfer for the lid to about 0.25 cm (¹/₁₀ in) and stick it over the sides with decalling fluid. Then, having removed the paper from the border decal, stretch it to fit snugly around the overlap both widthways and lengthways so that the design joins perfectly where it meets. When the transfer, or decal, has dried, any paper remaining on the surface can be re-dampened and rubbed off more easily once there is a solid backing to work against. Finally the transfer can be painted or antiqued, as you would with conventional decoupage.

3 Trim transfer to be slightly larger than the surface it has to cover; apply a coat of decalling fluid to the item, gently stretching the transfer to fit the area. Fix on with the shiny side down, previously papered side upwards.

PREPARING SURFACES

Once you have chosen the prints for your design, the surface of the object needs to be prepared. Choosing the prints beforehand enables you to select the base colour with the final colour scheme in mind. There are many different finishes too, which add to the detail of your finished item, but before attempting any decorative paint effects you must prepare the surface. This stage is crucial if your finished project is to be long-lasting enough to become an heirloom! The most important thing to remember is that each coat of primer/undercoat, paint, sealer, glue and varnish must adhere properly to the previous one. This is usually achieved by 'keying' the surface with various grades of sandpaper used alternately, or with Wet and Dry (silicon carbide) paper. Furthermore, it is vital that you choose your products carefully and use them in the correct order. The various constituents react differently depending on the order in which they are applied. It is important that you understand the reasoning behind this, before you can determine the order for yourself.

HOW TO USE THE VARIOUS PRODUCTS
Throughout this book we use four basic mediums or 'families' of products, including paint, varnish and adhesives. Each contains a different solvent, which has its own idiosyncrasies.

Oil-based products are the strongest and most durable. They can be used over any of the other materials, but generally take at least 12 hours to dry so tend to slow down the process considerably. The solvent in oil-based products is white spirit or turpentine, so the fumes are quite strong. It is therefore advisable only to use oil-based products in a well-ventilated area. Oil-based varnishes are golden and look like thin honey, they tend to turn yellow over time, particularly if many coats have been used. Any substance that advises you to clean brushes with white spirit after use is an oil-based one.

Water-based products are now being evolved that are almost as durable as oil-based ones; in general, they are less brittle and more elastic. Water-based varnishes have a milky appearance until dry and have little or no smell. They dry very quickly, which is useful, however, as a result tend to leave brush-marks. The brushes should be rinsed in water after use. Water-based products do not 'yellow' and can be used over spirit-based products, but not usually over oil-based ones as water does not adhere to oil. Water-based products include acrylic primer/undercoat, acrylic eggshell, emulsion – matt and silk – acrylic varnish, artist acrylic mediums, acrylic tube paints, and all PVA glues.

Spirit-based products have methylated spirit (or meths) as their main constituent; and are soluble with this medium, even when dry. They harden quickly to a brittle finish, are easy to sand and can be used over oil- or water-based products, so are useful to form a barrier between different mediums. Because they are meths-soluble, any subsequent coats of the same substance must be applied reasonably quickly, without overworking it too much, otherwise the previous coat will start to dissolve and come away. Shellac, a treacle-coloured lacquer, is a spirit-based product. It is useful for tinting and sealing new wood and MDF, and also for giving a painted finish a streaky antique appearance or the colours in your decoupage design an aged look; sanding sealer, knotting, white polish and transparent lacquer are all different versions of shellac: some bleached, some with additives, some glossy, some mid-sheen.

Cellulose-based products include car spray paints and one-coat metal paints, such as 'Smootherite', for use on metal surfaces. Car spray paints must not be used over oil-based paints as they cause them to crack and dissolve, but they can be used under oil-based products and either under or over water- or spirit-based products.

UNDERCOATS

If an object is to be painted or re-painted, there are three advantages to giving it an undercoat first: to help 'even' the surface; to start covering up the previous colour; and to bond each subsequent coat of paint.

PAINTED ITEMS

If the object you intend to decoupage is painted, it should be cleaned with sugar soap. If re-painting the surface it must be 'keyed' with a medium-grade sandpaper so that the next coat of paint grips properly; if this is not done there is a danger of subsequent coats chipping. Then it should be given a coat of primer and/or undercoat, which can be oil- or water-based, depending on what the next coat will be, how durable it needs to be and how long you are prepared to wait for it to dry. In most cases, I prefer to use the quick-drying water-based acrylic primer/undercoat, which can be followed by any kind of paint: oil-, water-, spirit- or cellulose-based. There are several oil-based primers, the strongest of which is aluminium primer.

UNTREATED WOOD

For new or stripped wood seal with acrylic primer/undercoat, or, if you wish to leave the natural wood showing in the background, seal with shellac or knotting. Shellac gives new wood a pleasant honey colour and knotting seals without changing the colour of the wood. Whichever medium you choose lightly sand with fine-grade sandpaper when dry.

STAINING

Alternatively, the bare wood can be stained before sealing, so that the stain sinks into the wood. For darker wood shades, use one of the ready-made oil-based or spirit-based stains in Walnut, Antique Pine or Mahogany. For other colours, dilute emulsion with four-five parts of water, paint on sparingly and allow to dry before sealing with sanding sealer.

WAXED SURFACES

Any wax must be removed from a surface otherwise the subsequent coat of paint, or glue, will not adhere to it. Either use a proprietary de-waxing solution and follow the instructions, or apply white spirit to the waxed surface on a piece of fine wire wool, allow it to soak in for a while to dissolve the wax and then rub using the wire wool, with the grain, until the wax appears on it. Repeat until all the wax has been removed. Wipe with warm soapy water and allow to dry. If it is still waxy, you may need to use a paint stripper.

Any piece that has been French-polished or varnished will, again, need to be 'keyed' using sandpaper, or Wet and Dry paper. Start with a medium- to coarse-grade sandpaper to remove most of the varnish and finish with a finer grade, always rubbing with the grain.

METAL OR ENAMEL SURFACES

Always begin by cleaning off any rust with a wire brush and Wet and Dry paper and coat either with Red Oxide metal primer, or one or two coats of rustproof cellulose-based paint. If you use Red Oxide metal primer follow with an oil-based undercoat and one or two coats of mid-sheen oil-based paint, allowing each coat at least 12 hours to dry. Using cellulose-based paint is a quicker method, but the alternative technique is a more durable one.

BASE COATS

When the undercoat is dry, sand lightly with fine-grade sandpaper, feeling the surface with your hand simultaneously until it is smooth. Beware not to sand too much on the edges or all the undercoat will be removed. In most cases one coat of oil- or water-based paint will be enough if it is well applied. Brush paint on a section in all directions, sparingly and quickly, using both sides of the brush to cover the whole area, then lightly stroke it in one direction. Repeat with next section. It is much better to apply two thin coats of paint, rather than having to sand down ugly runs. If the brush-strokes are very obvious when dry, they must be lightly sanded down.

For the base colour under decoupage I try,

whenever possible, to use water-based emulsions, matt or silk finish. To avoid having to buy lots of different colour paints, it is possible to choose about five basic shades plus white, which, by careful mixing, will give you endless possibilities. I suggest a brownish shade of red, a cold blue (without a hint of green), a middle yellow (not too green and not too orange) and a pretty, slightly emerald green, added to this some white and a Raw Umber, or similar dark brown, for a comprehensive palette. Possible combinations are: green plus yellow, plus a tiny amount of red for a lightened olive green; green again, plus the same amount of blue, with a little Raw Umber for a subtle antique greeny-blue. To lighten any colour, simply add a little white, remember that emulsions always dry darker than they appear when wet, so you may need to add more white than you imagine. By adding Raw Umber to any colour it immediately looks aged and more subtle.

FINISHES FOR PAINTED SURFACES

When the top coat or coats are dry you have the choice of whether to break the surface with a 'finish', or to leave it flat colour. Following is a variety of different paint finishes.

SPONGING

A simple broken colour surface, such as sponging, can look very effective, either on its own as a background, or with a coat of crackle varnish over the decoupage (*see pages 37–9*). To sponge over water-based emulsion or acrylic eggshell paint, mix the base colour with another emulsion or artists' acrylic tube paint to a slightly darker or lighter shade, using one part paint to four or five parts water. Stir well, then brush a little of the paint onto a natural sponge. Dab off most of the paint onto a paper towel, then lightly pat the surface with the sponge, frequently re-angling it to avoid a repeat pattern. When dry, after about 30 minutes, seal the surface with water-based varnish to make it less absorbent when glue is applied. For a more transparent effect, mix emulsion with two parts water and four to six parts water-based varnish, depending on the level of transparency you wish to achieve.

DRAGGING

This technique gives another pretty textured effect and can be achieved by painting an 'emulsion glaze' over water-based paint. All emulsion is opaque, but by mixing it with water-based glaze it gives a less solid, and softer, colour. To make an emulsion glaze, mix one part emulsion, or acrylic tube paint,

FAR LEFT. *Here, a pale coral emulsion, is sponged over the darker coral base coat. The paler shade was achieved simply by adding some white emulsion and water to the original base colour.*

LEFT. *Here a water-based scumble glaze, tinted with Hooker's Green acrylic tube paint, has been applied over a pale turquoise emulsion base then dragged with the grain. The effect is an attractive dark green with the light of the blue shining through, giving a far more interesting effect than the solid green alone.*

with the same amount of emulsion glaze, water-based varnish or white waterproof water-based (PVA) glue, such as Evostik wood glue or Uni-bond, this stretches the paint and makes it more transparent. Gradually add two to four parts water to this mixture, testing it regularly until you achieve the desired effect. Because the glaze dries quickly it needs to be dragged on in parallel lines, running the length of each facet. If the result is not streaky enough, you can quickly run a dry brush through the glaze before it dries to accentuate the lines. Leave to dry for about 30 minutes. Alternatively a water-based 'scumble' glaze (*see glossary*) can be used, mixed with emulsion or tinted with acrylic or gouache tube paint, this dries much more slowly (about 2–4 hours), allowing time to put it on all directions and then drag it with the grain. Use the same brush or a clean one for a more defined effect.

BAGGING

'Bagging' is one of the easiest finishes to achieve; simply pat a crumpled plastic bag over wet scumble glaze to give the effect of crushed velvet. Either an oil- or water-based scumble glaze can be used: oil-based over oil-based paint, water-based over emulsion or acrylic eggshell. An oil-based glaze can be tinted with oil tube paints and a water-based with acrylics. In the illustration below the

background colour is lighter than the glaze but, to bag a lighter colour over a darker one, just add a little white paint to the glaze. Providing the glaze is significantly lighter or darker than the background it will show. Paint the glaze on in all directions, then crumple the bag into a soft ball with plenty of creases and pat the wet glaze, again re-angling frequently to avoid a repetitive pattern. The thicker the bag, the bigger impression it will make. If the bag has writing on it, turn it inside out, as the print may dissolve in an oil-based glaze. If the effect is too dramatic at first, re-bag the surface with a clean area of plastic to soften the effect.

DISTRESSING

For an authentic aged, or 'distressed', look simply rub the painted surface with a medium-grade sandpaper in all the places where paint may have worn off over the years – the edges and wherever else it may have been handled. Either rub through to the undercoat, or right through to the wood, or whatever lies beneath. Always rub in one direction, 'going with the grain'. New wood must be sealed with shellac or sanding sealer, then painted with one coat of emulsion and left to dry. When sanded this will allow the wood to show through. To reveal the colour of the undercoat, two coats should be applied before the contrasting top coat.

RIGHT. *Equal amounts of Crimson and Burnt Umber acrylic tube paints were mixed with three times the quantity of water-based scumble glaze and painted over the base coat. The surface was then patted with a plastic bag. To get into the corners, use the edge of the bag.*

FAR RIGHT. *One coat of bright blue emulsion was painted over two coats of acrylic primer/undercoat, allowed to dry and then distressed, by rubbing with medium-grade sandpaper, going with the grain to reveal the white undercoat.*

WAX-DISTRESSING

For a slightly more defined distressed look, use a white candle to rub random streaks and drifts on each facet of the object you are decorating and on all the edges, again going with the grain. Quite hard pressure is needed to rub enough wax on in order to resist the paint. Again, apply the wax in the logical places where paint would have worn off over the years. Then paint on a contrasting coloured emulsion and, when dry, rub gently with fine-grade sandpaper. The top coat will come away quite easily where it was painted over the wax because it does not adhere to it. When you have finished sanding some of the wax may remain on the surface: this must be removed before sticking as glue will not adhere to it, so, either wipe the surface with white spirit, which is a wax-solvent, or seal the whole surface with sanding sealer.

METHS RUBBING

For an alternative effect, instead of trying to make the emulsion appear as smooth as possible, the paint can be brushed on so that the brush-strokes *do* show. Three coats of emulsion should be applied quite generously, drying between coats, then, when the final coat is dry, a deeper-coloured emulsion, mixed with four to five parts water, should be painted on sparingly.

When dry, the surface colour can be partly removed using a paper towel moistened with methylated spirit, rather than sandpaper. Because meths is the solvent for dry emulsion it removes the top layer, leaving the darker colour in the crevices made by the brush-strokes. Keep wetting the paper towel with meths and moving onto another area, going over the darkest areas later when dry, otherwise the emulsion base coat will start to dissolve. Alternatively a lighter colour can be used over a dark one: white over black can look very elegant as a background for black and white prints.

FAR LEFT. *(i) After sealing with shellac, or acrylic primer/undercoat, a coat of brown emulsion was painted on. This will only just be seen when the distressing is completed. When dry, streaks and drifts were made in the logical places all over the object, pressing firmly with a candle.*

FAR LEFT. *(ii) A contrasting coat of emulsion was then applied over the wax and allowed to dry. The top coat was distressed by rubbing with medium-grade sandpaper to reveal the colour below. The surface was wiped with white spirit to remove remaining wax.*

LEFT. *Having painted on three coats of acrylic primer/undercoat thickly, a thin coat of Raw Umber emulsion, diluted with five parts water, was applied sparingly. When dry, the surplus was removed with methylated spirit.*

SMOOTHING SURFACES

To create a really smooth surface for decoupage and/or gilding you can use gesso – a fine chalky powder. This is mixed with 'rabbit skin' size to the consistency of cream. Several coats are applied to the surface, sanded with fine-grade sandpaper until smooth then burnished with 0000 wire wool. This is time-consuming so a thick water-based paint, such as distemper- or casein-bound paint, makes an excellent alternative.

For a very smooth surface, similar to meths rubbing (*see page 23*) casein paint or distemper can be used, instead of gesso, together with Raw Umber. Paint three coats over the initial coat of acrylic primer/undercoat, applying it with the grain, thickly enough for the brush-strokes to show, and dry between coats. This builds up a layer similar to gesso. Next, sparingly paint over a glaze of Raw Umber oil tube paint mixed with white spirit to the consistency of olive oil. Wipe the surface gently with some white spirit on a paper towel, again going with the grain, to blend in the oil glaze and push it deeper into the layers of soft paint. Allow this to soak in and dry overnight. Sand the surface with fine-grade sandpaper until smooth and nearly light enough in colour, then burnish with 0000 wire wool to a fine patina.

If the base coat is a plain matt emulsion colour, or a water-based finish, you can seal the surface, when dry, with satin water-based varnish to give it a sheen. This makes it less absorbent, enabling you to re-position the cut-outs more easily than if sticking straight onto a matt surface. Water-based varnish dries quickly and can leave brush-strokes, so apply it sparingly and quickly (*see page 40*).

PAINT FINISHES ON GLASS AND CHINA

To decoupage straight onto glass or china no preparation is normally necessary, providing you use a strong PVA glue, wood glue, for example. Do make sure that you wash the surface thoroughly with warm soapy water and dry it well before sticking decoupage motifs. This eliminates any dirt or marks on the surface.

You can paint china or porcelain with either oil- or water-based ceramic paint. Emulsion can be used too, but to make it stick, the surface must first be 'keyed' with a coat of PVA glue, diluted with water to the consistency of paint, or a water-based varnish strong enough to adhere to metal or china. The water-based ceramic paints lend themselves well to creating a mottled background colour, achieved by sponging on drifts of various shades.

SPONGING ON CHINA
Mix the water-based ceramic paint with a little water, dampen a natural sponge and paint a little of the mixture on to it. Dab on your chosen colour in diagonal drifts of differing sizes, leaving small gaps between them. Next, mix a lighter, darker or slightly different shade and sponge that on, in between and overlapping the initial drifts. Several colours can be applied, one after another, sponging lightly not to disturb the water-soluble drifts that are already there. When dry, it should be fired in an ordinary oven, following the instructions on the ceramic paint, then sealed with an oil-based varnish.

FAR RIGHT. *After sponging two or three shades of greeny-blue onto this white china lamp-base, an aluminium bronze powder, which is silver in colour, was added to the water-based ceramic paint diluted with water and painted onto the sponge. It was then applied lightly in drifts for a lustrous effect.*

MARBLING ON GLASS OR CHINA

Wonderful effects can be achieved on both glass and china using transparent spirit-based lacquer (or French enamel varnish). This is available in various colours or translucent for you to tint yourself with powdered spirit aniline dyes. The powders are very toxic, so it is essential to wear a protective mask and rubber gloves when working with them (*see right*). For a see-through marbly effect sprinkle small amounts of powdered aniline dyes on lacquered glass or china before it dries using a fitch or toothbrush. Then swab the surface with a paper towel soaked in methylated spirit to dissolve the dyes and create drifts of colour. Little holes can be opened up by spattering the surface with meths. Even when dry the surface can be re-moistened and adjusted again and again until you are happy with the result. The methylated spirit used to blend the aniline dyes has a tendency to dissolve water-based varnish needed to seal decoupage underneath (*see page 17*).

1 *Paint the underside of your plate with transparent lacquer to make it sticky. Dip a fitch or toothbrush into the powdered dye and pick up a **very** small amount. Then sprinkle randomly onto the surface in each of your chosen colours, by gently tapping your brush.*

WHAT YOU WILL NEED
Mask and rubber gloves. Glass plate (or any glass/china object). Transparent lacquer. Paintbrush. A selection of different coloured aniline dyes. Fitch or toothbrush. Methylated spirit. Paper towel.

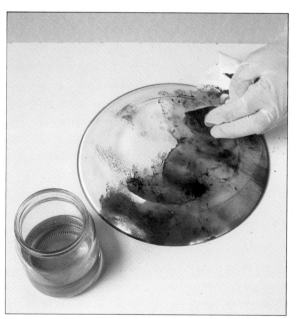

2 *Dampen a piece of paper towel with plenty of methylated spirit and pat this all over the sticky surface. This dissolves and blends the dyes. Re-moisten your paper towel frequently with meths to keep the surface wet and prevent the lacquer drying and sticking to the paper.*

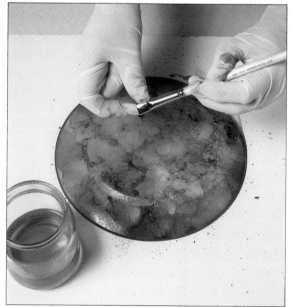

3 *Spatter the darkest areas with meths by flicking it from your fitch. This opens up lighter pools of colour in the blended drifts. Continue until happy with the effect. You must wear rubber gloves and mask from the outset when using these dyes.*

PAINTING FREEHAND LINES

A painted line or border around the edge of the item you are decoupaging forms an effective finishing touch. If, however, you are unaccustomed to freehand painting this can be a difficult task. Here are some tips which should help. When I first started painting straight lines, I used to stick two strips of ordinary masking tape down leaving a gap between them for the line. This is quite a time-consuming method because the tape is difficult to apply and has the annoying habit of allowing the paint to seep under its edges a little, reducing the clarity of the line; worse still, when removing the tape, sometimes the base coat comes away with it. If you choose to use masking tape as a technique for painting lines, buy a low-tack tape and, before you use it, decrease its stickiness by fleetingly sticking a length to cotton clothing. Hopefully this will prevent it from removing the paint.

Another way of painting a straight line is to place a piece of picture-frame moulding on the surface to act as a guide. You can use this to steady your hand or the brush as you are painting. It is important to use the raised inside edge of the moulding to guide you because this does not touch the surface and cause the paint to run.

Alternatively, if you have the correct brush, it is not difficult to paint a completely freehand line. Straight ones are the easiest, but with a little practice, a curved one for a circular object is possible too. For these lines, a brush called a 'coachliner', or 'stripper', is used; they are available in various lengths, from 1.5 cm to 5 cm ($\frac{1}{2}$ to 2 in). The shortest ones are used for short straight lines and small curves, the longest for long straight lines. The hairs are all the same length, which prevents the line from getting thicker or thinner at any point as it would with a normal watercolour brush; and, being long, it tends to hold paint rather like a fountain pen.

When using a lining brush make a puddle of paint large enough to cover the length of your brush. Use either a coloured acrylic

1 A puddle of acrylic tube paint or emulsion, large enough to fit the length of the brush, was mixed with a little water on a plate then the dampened bristles of the 5 cm (2 in) lining brush were laid in it and turned over to absorb as much paint as possible.

2a Using a piece of picture-frame moulding, with raised edge turned in towards the intended line, as a guide, a straight line is painted with a long-haired lining brush. Fingers but not the bristles should be touching the inside edge of the moulding.

tube paint and a little white paint to bind it diluted with water, or use emulsion mixed with water to the consistency of cream. Moisten the brush with water, then lie the whole length of the bristles in the paint and draw the brush towards you; turn the brush over and repeat until all the bristles are covered as far as the metal join, or 'ferrule'.

LONG LINES

It is a good idea to practise painting a freehand line on a piece of card before you attempt the real thing, as starting and finishing the line can take a little practice. To paint long lines, on a piece of furniture for example, it is essential to stand, placing one foot in front of the other about a pace apart, as near as possible to the point at which the line is to finish. Put your weight onto the front foot and lean forward, stretching out so that you can reach the start of the line. Hold the brush as you would a pen (*see opposite*), or cradle it in your upturned hand, thumb on top to steady it, knuckles touching the surface to guide you. Place the tip of the brush in one corner, a little

way in from the edge and the same distance down from the corner. The nearer the line is to an edge, the easier it is to judge the distance by eye and so keep the line straight as you are painting it. Gently lower the length of the bristles until two-thirds lie on the surface in a straight line. If you hold the brush like a pen, stick your little finger out for balance, then draw the brush towards you, keeping a constant distance from the edge. Gradually move your weight from the front foot to the back, rather than moving your arm or elbow, and when you see the end approaching start to lift the brush up slowly, still moving down the line, so that just the tip is lifted off at the end. Always have a damp cloth at your side, so that if the line wavers or goes too far it can be wiped off before it dries. (If the line gets too dry to rub off with a damp cloth, try a little methylated spirit, or simply paint over it with the base colour.)

For very long lines it may be necessary to lift the brush off carefully in the middle, reload with paint and continue the line, overlapping the end of the previous brush-stroke.

SHORT LINES

Shorter lines, between 20 and 30 cm (8 and 12 in), can be done sitting down, but still using a long brush. Shorter brushes should be used for lines under 20 cm or for small curves. With a little practice you will soon find which length brush suits each job best. If you find painting curves harder, try drawing a light pencil or chalk line, measured in from the edge with a ruler, to guide you.

When all the lines are dry, go over them again to correct the odd wobble, and also to add definition and make them look even.

GOLD LINES

For gilded lines, either use the methods mentioned above using gold paint – water-based acrylic is the best because it is thinner than oil-based, which tends to run if varnished with oil-based varnish. Alternatively paint a line with gold size and apply thin strips of Dutch metal leaf (a little wider than the line) smoothing them flat with a soft-haired brush, and allowing them to dry before removing the surplus leaf (*see pages 32–5*).

2b *Using a shorter-bristled lining brush for curved lines, fill it up to the ferrule with paint, the little finger supporting the hand on the edge of the tray. The line is very close to the edge, which acts as a guide, making it easier to paint evenly.*

CUTTING TECHNIQUES

Once you have decided on the theme for your project and chosen the designs, it is best to cut out the various pieces roughly with a pair of straight scissors. Then, using a small pair of curved nail-scissors, you should cut right on, or just inside, the edge of each detail using the tips of the blades to cut into small indentations, turning the paper with the other hand as you do so. If possible hold the scissors underneath the paper, angling the lower blade in towards the paper so that the cut edge is bevelled; this avoids a stark white edge. If a design has internal areas to be cut, they should be done first, by piercing the centre with the point of one blade and carefully cutting outwards from the hole.

Black and white prints often have delicate 'fronds' which are too fine to cut around; they should be reinstated with a thin-nibbed black waterproof pen before cutting, or removed completely and painted in once the design is stuck. If the design is so flimsy that it might be damaged by cutting around all the intricate details, you can leave small paper 'bridges' to support them (*see below left*). When cutting long thin stems, which are vulnerable if cut in one length, divide each stem into sections, but remember the order in which they join together! If you are using a scalpel, always cut from the indentations outwards.

CUTTING BORDERS

If your design has borders, these should be stuck first in order to achieve the correct balance. Borders which join at an angle need to be 'mitred' at the corners in order to join the two strips at an angle. To mitre a corner the border design for each side should be cut about 5 cm (2 in) longer than the edge it is intended for depending on its width. If the border has a repeat pattern it must be centred on each edge so that the design matches at the corners. Then only the central area of each section should be stuck, leaving the overlaps free at each end. Placing a ruler precisely through the angles where the borders cross, cut through them with a craft knife from the inside outwards. Remove surplus paper, lift up the flaps, paint glue on and stick.

To curve a straight border, use a design with rounded details that can be snipped in between to ease them around the curve. When cutting out, allow a little more border than necessary at either end. Always leave the first 2.5 cm (1 in) of paper intact; then snip between the segments of detail in the next inch and glue this section firmly to your surface, easing the segments around the curve. Repeat an inch at a time, and when almost complete decide where to join the two ends by 'butting' or overlapping them.

RIGHT. *Because the spiral design of this baroque motif is so delicate, small paper bridges have been left in strategic positions to give the cut-out strength. Once the central areas have been stuck down they can be snipped off and the flimsy ends they were attached to carefully stuck into place.*

Large cut-outs have a tendency to wrinkle when they are stuck down, so it is advisable to divide groups of motifs into the smallest cut-outs possible. If you do need to use a larger, less intricate shape, it is easier to cut it out with sharp pointed scissors with longer blades; these give a cleaner edge because you do not need to snip so often. Remember that the more accurate the cutting the better the finished item will look.

MITRING CORNERS

1 Mark the centre of each edge. Cut strips of border 5 cm (2 in) longer than necessary and centre each one on the mark already made. Glue the centre down leaving the ends free.

2 Place a ruler across each corner and cut from the inside of the angle outwards with a craft knife, pressing firmly on the ruler. Glue ends and stick in place.

CURVING STRAIGHT BORDERS

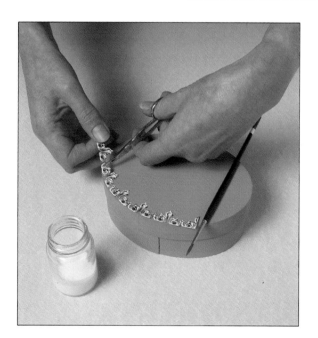 

1 Leave first 2.5 cm (1in) of border unstuck. Snip between segments of next inch on the inside; cutting about halfway through the width of the border. Stick this in place.

2 Snip and glue each section in turn, easing around the curve. Stick down. Overlap segments on inside of border until ends meet, choosing the best place to butt or join them.

ARRANGING AND STICKING

Always experiment with the arrangement of your cut-outs before sticking them down. Use a tiny ball of Blu-Tack on the back of each motif to position it temporarily. Sometimes the design falls into place immediately, but other times, even after several attempts, it refuses to hang together. The best solution in these instances is to leave the project for a few days.

Remember that the space left around and between the motifs in a design is as important as the cut-outs themselves. Too many motifs clustered together with no space around them and your design will look claustrophobic, too few and the design will be lost.

OVERLAPPING CUT-OUTS

If you wish to overlap motifs rather than leave space between them. Arrange the cut-outs as before with Blu-Tack, but when you stick them be sure to stick the undermost pieces first. To do this you will have to remove the top layer, or layers; once a piece has been lifted from the design it is amazingly difficult to remember where it went. To avoid this, either do a rough sketch of the design before you dismantle it, or draw around each piece with chalk. This should enable you to replace your motifs in more or less the correct place.

BORDERS

To make a wide border from a variety of cut-outs in different shapes and sizes, which is roughly the same width all the way around, mark inner and outer lines with chalk at the maximum width you require. This will provide an area within which you can arrange your motifs in the knowledge that you will end up with an even border (*see page 96, step 6*).

1 These pieces of diamond jewellery could be arranged in various designs.. Here a brooch and four earrings were arranged in a cross and surrounded by a border of swags and pearls, fixing them with Blu-Tack.

2 As an alternative way of arranging the same motifs, which I find more pleasing, the earrings can be used to form the border. The pearls and diamond swags now form a design for the sides of the box.

USING TEMPLATES

When arranging designs on circular or cylindrical objects, it is important that the elements are equally spaced. To do this accurately use a template or guide-lines.

It is best to mark all guide-lines in chalk because it is so easy to adjust and wipe off.

Pencil can dent the surface and, worse still, damage the decoupage when you rub it out. If you must use pencil choose a soft, preferably blunt, one. You can use pencil marks when you intend to cover them up with cut-outs, to help centre them for example.

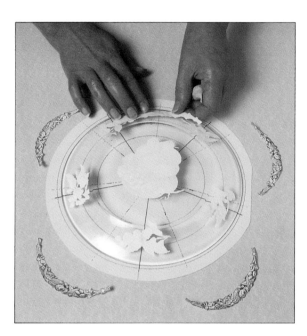

FAR LEFT. *To place a design around a circular object, use a template to mark on equal segments. If the object is glass like this plate, you can simply use the visible lines to guide you. This project has been divided into five segments: personally, I like the effect of an uneven number of segments.*

LEFT. *When decoupaging on the outside of a glass jar it is very useful to draw your design onto a piece of paper, which fits exactly around the inside of the jar, and use this as a guide. This helps to get things level.*

STICKING MOTIFS

Every bit of paper should adhere to the surface beneath, otherwise air may get trapped and will 'bubble' when you begin varnishing. The glue you use is dependent on three factors: the type of paper being used, whether or not it is sealed and the style of the design.

Waterproof or water-soluble PVA (polyvinyl acetate) glue is suitable for most projects. The water-soluble variety allows cut-outs to be soaked off, even when dry. Diluting these glues with a little water will make it easier to paint on, but do not dilute it when using on glass or china.

Use a watercolour paintbrush to paint the glue sparingly on the back of your motif. If you apply too much it will ooze out when the motif is stuck down. Paint the glue on from the centre outwards, ensuring that the whole print is covered. Put it lightly in place immediately and make any adjustments, then press firmly from the centre outwards with your fingers using a paper towel to soak up any surplus glue. Do not rub as this can damage the print. Finally check that all the edges are securely stuck as it is easy to miss them with the glue. For larger or very intricate cut-outs apply glue in strips, starting with a central one and work outwards in parallel strips.

Very thin or absorbent paper is almost impossible to stick without wrinkling. To avoid this you can use liquid gum arabic, which dries slowly, applied to your object rather than the cut-out. Paint a facet with it and arrange your motifs while it is still wet. If any part fails to adhere just re-paint it with the gum arabic. This type of glue can cause subsequent coats of some water-based varnish to crack, so always seal it with a methylated spirit-based lacquer like sanding sealer or oil-based varnish. This method is not very successful with prints that have already been sealed, as they do not adhere well.

GILDING

Gold leaf has been popular for thousands of years and its splendour still holds a fascination for many today. Waterlaying gold leaf requires experience and is probably best left to the experts. Oil or mordant gilding, however, is much easier to do and with a little practice can be accomplished by us all. For both these methods the leaf is stuck on with a glue called gold size, for oil gilding we use an oil-based size and for mordant gilding we use a water-based size.

Dutch Metal leaf, also known as Schlag, is a type of imitation gold, made from copper and zinc. It is much less expensive than real gold leaf, and therefore makes a practical alternative for inexperienced gilders. Dutch Metal leaf is a little thicker than gold leaf so is easier to handle. It comes in books of 25 sheets: each sheet is 14 sq cm (5½ sq in) and can be bought loose-leaved between sheets of rouge paper, or in transfer form (attached to thin waxed paper) which is much easier to handle and pre-cut with scissors.

GETTING STARTED

The smoother the surface prior to gilding the more professional the end result will look. There are various techniques for creating a smooth surface (*see page 24*), but if you merely wish to gild small details, regular emulsion sanded to a smooth finish will suffice.

Traditionally gold is waterlaid over a coloured base – red/brown or Yellow Ochre or black – so that when it is burnished a glimpse of the base colour shows through. Oil or mordant gilding cannot be burnished, but it is still a good idea to use a reddish-brown emulsion underneath, in case any hair-line cracks appear, or should you wish to distress it.

USING GOLD SIZE

Oil-based gold size is a little thicker than oil-based varnish and more honey-coloured. A coat of size is applied sparingly to the object and allowed to dry until just tacky; the drier it is, the brighter the gold will be. Gold size comes in a variety of drying times: 1-hour, 3-hour and 12-hour. The time indicates how long it takes to reach the tackiness required before applying the leaf. It will feel dry when lightly stroked, but just sticky when pressed with the knuckle. It should remain workable for the same length of time again.

To speed things up water-based size can be used; this is known as mordant gilding. The size has a milky appearance, but loses this milkiness when it reaches the correct tackiness to lay leaf. It too should be applied as sparingly as possible. The advantage of water-based size over oil-based is that it can be used (*continued on page 34*)

WHAT YOU WILL NEED
Red/brown or black emulsion. Fine-grade sandpaper. A book of transfer Dutch Metal leaf. Water-based or oil-based gold size. Gold bronze powder. Straight scissors. Small paintbrush (for paint and size). Soft-haired brush or 'mop'.

GILDING WITH DUTCH METAL LEAF

PREPARATION

Paint the surface of your object with reddish-brown emulsion, or black if you prefer, so that any cracks that do occur in the leaf look intentional. When the paint is dry it should be sanded so that you have a perfectly smooth surface; any unevenness will show through the gilding. If the item you are gilding is particularly uneven you can paint the surface with gesso, distemper or casein and sand smooth before applying the emulsion. Then sparingly paint on a coat of gold size, water-based or oil-based, whichever you have chosen. Whilst this is drying to the correct tackiness for sticking, you can cut your gold leaf to size. Remove a sheet of leaf from the book, sliding it away from its protective sheet of rouge paper. Try not to touch the leaf with your fingers as this can cause marks from oxidization later on. Do not remove the backing but cut the sheet into pieces slightly larger than the areas they are destined to cover.

1 Holding the leaf by its backing, lower it onto the surface slowly, keeping it horizontal. Position the leaf carefully, as once it has touched the tacky surface it cannot be adjusted. Smooth over the greased paper with your fingers before gently removing it.

2 Cover each facet in this way, overlapping the edges by about 6 mm (¼ in). Then, starting with the last piece of leaf laid, smooth lightly over surface with a soft-haired brush or 'mop' to eliminate any tiny air bubbles and ensure that every square millimetre is stuck.

3 The edges may curl, but should be left intact whilst the size dries overnight. Then remove all loose bits of leaf with the side of the soft-haired brush, rotating it. Any holes in the leaf can be patched by re-applying size and leaf or by dabbing with bronze powder.

15–20 minutes after application and remains workable for at least 36 hours.

The advantage of oil-based size lies in the end result. Because it dries slowly, it levels out to give a smoother surface, whereas the quick-drying water-based size is more likely to show brush-marks through the leaf.

PATCHING

Should there be any holes or blemishes in your gilded surface all is not lost! They can be almost invisibly mended with the following technique. Simply cut a piece of leaf (still attached to its backing) a little larger than the hole it is intended to cover and press it firmly over the blemish before the size dries. Smooth over it with a mop, leaving the overlaps in place to dry overnight. Remove these with the rest of the surplus leaf. For hair-line cracks, to which a piece of leaf may not adhere, dab on a little matching gold bronze powder with a fine-haired brush, or a piece of velvet wound around your finger. Because the powder is so fine it will stick in tiny areas where the leaf might not. It is also useful to repair a messy join, revealed when tidying up the overlaps between sheets of leaf, or in the deep indentations of carved surfaces.

DISTRESSING GOLD LEAF

Once you have gilded your surface and tidied it the following day, you may decide that it is too bright for the design you had planned. If so, there are various ways of 'antiquing' or 'distressing' the leaf to make it look aged. The simplest way to achieve this effect is to rub the gilded surface with fine wire wool, lightly stroking in one direction – going with the grain, whether this is real or imaginary. If you were burnishing waterlaid leaf this would reveal the undercoat, but the layer of gold size required for oil or mordant gilding prevents this. Instead, grey streaks are revealed. To remove them, you merely need to moisten a paper towel with white spirit or turpentine and gently rub over the already distressed gilding, again going with 'the grain', to reveal the true undercoat.

For a slightly more uneven, random distressing, use just white spirit, or turpentine, on a piece of paper towel without using wire wool first. Rub gently in one direction over the gilding; this will remove the leaf and the size in spots and patches. The more you continue to rub, the more distressed it will look.

SEALING GOLD LEAF

Before decoupaging on top of gilding the leaf must be sealed ideally with lacquer or some water-based varnishes (if you wish to distress the gilded object do this first). Methylated spirit- or cellulose-based lacquers are the best products for this task, shellac or sanding sealer for instance. Oil-based varnish is not

RIGHT. *For a distressed effect, rub gently with fine wire wool, then stroke in one direction with white spirit on a paper towel. This is necessary to remove the size which shows up as grey beneath the distressed leaf.*

FAR RIGHT. *The entire surface of this tray was gilded over a coat of red/ brown emulsion. Whole sheets of Dutch Metal leaf were overlapped to cover the base, then smaller pieces were cut for the sides. After drying, all the surplus leaf was removed and the tray was given a coat of shellac.*

FAR LEFT. *Very small details can be gilded with metal leaf, but you must be very accurate when applying the size.*

LEFT. *If you are gilding curved or rounded surfaces, cut the leaf (whilst still attached to its backing) into rectangular pieces of the appropriate depth for your curve. Then cut these diagonally to give you wedge-shaped pieces, which will fit around the curve as shown here. Overlap each piece in the same way as before.*

recommended because the solvent it contains could damage the leaf if you brush it too much. Oil-based varnish also leaves the leaf with less of a gleam. When the sealer is totally dry, arrange and stick your decoupage design in the usual way using PVA glue, finishing with as many coats of sealer as necessary for its use.

GILDING DETAILS

To gild bevelled edges for instance, the size must be applied very accurately to the area you wish to gild. A square-ended sable brush, slightly narrower than the width of the detail, is a useful tool. This gives a more accurate line than a rounded watercolour brush. Cut the leaf to size and apply as before, overlapping each section. Leave overnight and tidy up when dry. Seal details only if you intend to decoupage directly over them, if not wait until the design is stuck and seal the whole item in one go.

GILDING ON GLASS

Gilding the underside of glass plates, bowls or even frames can give another exciting effect (*see right*). If you are using decoupage and another paint effect, complete them first and seal the entire surface with water-based varnish. When the varnish is dry, apply the gold size over the whole area and attach the leaf as instructed on page 33 when the size

has reached the correct tackiness.

When dry, the leaf will need to be tidied up and then the whole surface given a coat of shellac or sanding sealer to protect the leaf and to help the next coat of paint adhere to the leaf, followed when dry with a coat of oil-based paint. This does not show through the metal leaf so any colour can be used. Black is the most usual, but you may wish to choose a colour that matches your decoupage design. Leave this to dry overnight and then seal again with several coats of oil-based varnish to make the item waterproof.

LEFT. *These two glass plates have been decoupaged on the underside and sealed with water-based varnish. The one on the left has been given a marble effect with lacquer and aniline dyes (see page 25) over the decoupage. Then both have been gilded.*

MARBLED GILDING

If you want to be adventurous, a really beautiful effect can be achieved by applying fragments of gold leaf over a painted surface. A striking effect can be achieved with a contrasting coloured background, such as black, or for a more subtle effect, a colour closer to gold, such as yellow or orange, can be used. This effect can also be used under glass with stunning results. When gilding under glass you must stick your decoupage design beforehand and gild on top of it. When dry always seal the leaf with spirit-based lacquer.

PREPARATION

For this marbled effect, loose-leaf, rather than transfer, is required as it must be crumpled in the hand before applying it. When the painted base coat is dry or the decoupage designs firmly stuck and given a coat of water-based varnish if under glass, cover the whole surface with gold size and leave it to become tacky before applying the leaf.

1 Lightly crumple a sheet of loose Dutch Metal leaf in your hand. Attach it to a corner of the surface and, holding it gently, draw away. Zig zag across the surface, feeding the leaf through your index finger and thumb, simultaneously patting it erratically onto the surface.

2 When completed, much of the leaf will still be unattached. To flatten the surface, cover the whole area, section by section, with greaseproof paper. Smooth all over with your hand, getting into all the crevices and flattening the crumpled leaf beneath.

3 Gently rub the entire surface in a circular motion with a damp natural sponge. Continue until the surface is as smooth as possible with little veins showing. Dry overnight then seal with water- or spirit-based varnish before sticking the designs.

CREATING AN ANTIQUE LOOK

To give your decoupaged item an antique look you can 'age' it, either by making the varnish look cracked or by making the colours look faded. The easiest way to age decoupage is to tint it with shellac or paint it with brown emulsion, simply brushing it on and wiping it off quickly with a paper towel, leaving the paint in the ridges (*see page 57, step 2*). The crackled look, although more complicated and time-consuming, is probably most popular. Crackles are created by applying two types of glue, one over the other, which react together causing the cracks. The first layer is a slow-drying oil-based adhesive – 3-hour gold size, and the second is a quick-drying water-based glue – liquid gum arabic. Despite the fact that two types of glue are used to create this effect the common term for it is 'crackle varnishing'. To make the cracks show, oil tube paint (in a contrasting colour to the background) has to be rubbed well into the cracks and then varnished over. Proprietary brands of crackle varnish are available from good art supply shops.

CRACKLE VARNISHING

Crackle varnish should be applied towards the end of the varnishing process. There are two reasons for this: firstly, several coats of varnish will lessen the ridge around the paper cut-outs and reduce the risk of oil-paint, used to define the cracks, gathering around them; secondly, because the top coat of crackle varnish is water-soluble even when dry, only oil-based varnish can be used over it. Oil-based varnish is slower drying than water-based, therefore to save time use as many coats of water-based varnish as possible first. Because the initial coat of crackle varnish is oil-based it will happily go over any other medium.

APPLYING CRACKLE VARNISH

When the varnish is dry, sparingly apply the first layer of crackle varnish – the 3-hour gold size. Dip your brush into the size about a quarter to one-third of the way up the bristles. Place the brush somewhere near the middle of one side, or facet, and spread the size as thinly as possible in all directions, almost scrubbing it into the surface. Hold it up to the light and check that the whole section is covered, the reflection will reveal any bits that have been missed. Repeat over the adjacent sections, smoothing the varnish back lightly into the previous section each time with the tip of the brush. Once the whole surface is covered, check again that no areas are left untouched, by holding it up to the light, and allow to dry until barely tacky. It should feel dry when lightly stroked and just tacky when pressed with the fingertips. Do not rush the second coat, it is always better to let the size dry too much than not enough.

It can take anything from $1\frac{1}{2}$-4 hours, or more, to reach the right tackiness depending on the temperature, humidity, how thickly the size has been applied and even the shape of the decoupaged object. So, always judge it by how tacky it feels. The drier it is before the second layer is applied, the finer the cracks will be. If in doubt, leave it longer! Even if the surface feels absolutely dry, cracks will still appear because oil-based products take about two weeks to dry completely.

When the size is dry enough the second layer – liquid gum arabic – can be applied. Again, spread on fairly sparingly and make sure that every bit is covered by holding it up to the light. The thickness of this coat is very important as it will affect the appearance of the cracks. If it is too thin, they will be close together and very shallow, and able to retain only a little of the oil-paint rubbed in. If it is too thick, it will take longer than 30 minutes to dry and the cracks will be wide and further apart. If you miss a bit, that area will appear much darker when the oil-paint is rubbed in as it will still be tacky.

This coat may open up a little along the brush-strokes. You can see them by holding it up to the light. If they are visible, smooth the surface lightly with the flats of your fingers in a circular motion until the varnish is nearly dry. This helps to eliminate the brush-strokes, evenly distribute the second coat and make it adhere better to the first coat. When all brush-marks are gone, stop rubbing.

The liquid gum arabic dries in about 20–30 minutes depending on its thickness. It is like the glue on stamps and envelopes, and does not dry properly in a damp or humid atmosphere. So ensure that you put it somewhere warm and damp-free. Although this second coat takes a comparatively short time to dry, ideally you should leave it at least overnight. This will allow the first coat to continue drying naturally; while doing so it shrinks, eventually causing the brittle top coat to crack. Again the longer you leave it the better the result will be. After part-drying naturally, apply gentle warmth to the surface with a hairdryer (or by placing near a radiator or another heat source) to accelerate the first coat's drying process and cause the cracks to appear.

If you are short of time, providing the top coat is dry to touch (approximately 30 minutes after applying it), you can use a hairdryer to achieve cracks instantly. There is a danger that this will make the first coat dry too quickly, giving larger cracks further apart; so delay warming as long as possible. Hold the hairdryer about 3–4 inches from the surface, moving it back and forth. If it gets too hot, wrinkles may occur, or worse still, the crackles may peel off. So be sure to warm it gradually for even crackles. It is difficult to see the cracks at this stage and you may think your efforts have been unsuccessful, but if you hold the piece up to the light you should be able to detect a fine cobweb effect. If you still cannot see them do not despair, they may be so fine that they are only visible after rubbing the oil-paint into them.

ANTIQUING THE CRACKS

To emphasize the cracks, oil tube paint must be worked into them; do not use acrylic tube paint because it is water-based and will dissolve the water-soluble layer that contains the cracks. Make a thick paste from your oil tube paint by mixing it with a little white spirit. Using a brush or a paper towel spread the paint all over your crackled item, rubbing in a circular motion so that it gets into all the cracks. Wipe off the surplus almost immediately with a clean piece of paper towel, so that the colour remains only in the cracks; repeat with a thicker mixture if they do not show enough. Leave this to dry overnight then seal with oil-based varnish.

RIGHT. After several coats of water-based varnish over the dried decoupage, two coats of crackle varnish were applied: first the 3-hour gold size and then liquid gum arabic. When the cracks had appeared they were made more visible by rubbing in Green Umber oil-paint. This tray could perhaps have benefitted from some additional coats of water-based varnish before crackle varnishing. As you can see the oil-paint has collected around the edges of the motifs as well as in the cracks.

FAR RIGHT. Mix oil tube paint with a little white spirit to make a paste and rub all over the surface of your crackled object with a cloth or brush in a circular motion. Then remove the surplus with paper kitchen towel, leaving the paint in the cracks only.

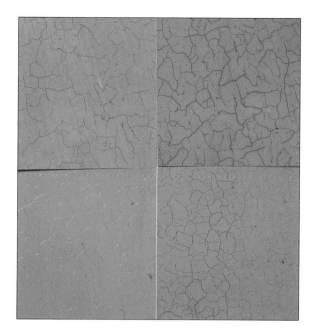

WHICH COLOUR?

The colour you rub into the cracks will affect the shade of the end result. Whatever the colour it must contrast with the background. To get the effect of dust built up over the ages, Raw Umber is generally used. Since this is a very yellow brown you will need to adjust your base colour by subtracting a bit of yellow because Raw Umber turns pale blue into turquoise and gives darker blues a green tinge; similarly it makes pink look coral. As it is a fairly light colour it works best over pale to medium shades.

Experiment with other shades of brown which are darker and warmer than Raw Umber and are effective over darker colours. Other colours, Payne's Grey for example – a blue-grey – age without yellowing. Alternatively ultramarine, mixed with a little black works well over a cold blue, particularly if you do not want it to turn green. Over dark colours such as black or dark green, cream or white are effective. You can even dust gold-bronze or aluminium powder into the cracks with a small brush for a metallic cobweb effect; because the gold size remains sticky for some time, the powder will adhere to it.

Different colour tube paints dry at different rates. Raw Umber for instance usually dries within 12 hours, but Payne's Grey can take more than three days. If you varnish the crackles too soon the paint will run and smear over the surface. The colour you use will dictate how long it takes to dry.

CORRECTING MISTAKES

Sometimes your attempts to crackle can fail; one of the most common problems is that the second coat of varnish does not completely cover the first. In this case the oil-paint will stick to the areas missed by the second coat, making dark scars which are very stubborn. If this should occur, put a little white spirit or turpentine onto a cotton wool bud or twisted bit of paper towel. Using this carefully rub the paint away from the affected areas. You will probably lose the crackles there, but at least the colour will match the rest of your item.

If your cracks are a total disaster, you can remove them with a damp cloth, because it is water-soluble, and start again. Even if you have already antiqued the cracks, you can remove the oil-paint with white spirit after you have removed the top coat. Alternatively, you can take a pan scrubber to the whole thing. In either case you need six coats of water-based varnish to protect your decoupage before crackling, otherwise removing the cracks could damage your design.

AGEING GOLD LEAF

Another way to antique a gilded, or varnished surface, with or without distressing it first, is to paint over it with Raw Umber emulsion. Metallic or varnished surfaces will resist water-based paint, so do not dilute it, unless it is very thick, or it will not adhere.

Over a flat gilded surface, drag the paint on sparingly in parallel sweeps using a brush, allow to half dry for a minute or two and wipe off the surplus in the same direction with paper towel. This gives a dragged effect similar to that achieved on the gilded 'ace' card box (*see page 73*). For a sponged look, pat firmly with crumpled paper towel while the paint is still wet.

If the surface under the leaf is slightly rough, paint a small section at a time and wipe off immediately. The brown paint will remain only in the uneven dips of the surface, like the candlestick on page 32. When dry it should be sealed with matt or satin water- or oil-based varnish.

FAR LEFT. *Here are four examples of crackle varnish using different coloured oil tube paint (and one example of bronze powder) over the same background colour. From top left, going clockwise, they are Raw Umber, Ultramarine, Payne's Grey and gold-bronze powder.*

VARNISHING

Whether or not you have crackled your decoupage project, the aim is to create a completely smooth surface with no ridges where the paper-edges are, creating the effect of inlay. Truly dedicated decoupers will give a piece anything from 30–100 coats of varnish to achieve this. You may find the prospect a little daunting, especially as a coat of oil-based varnish can take up to 24 hours to dry. Do not fear however, as there are short cuts!

If the item is unlikely to be handled frequently, like a clock-face or a mirror-frame, fewer coats of varnish are necessary than for a table-mat or a tray which must be both heat-resistant and thoroughly washable.

TYPES OF VARNISH

Varnishes, both water- and oil-based, are available in three finishes: gloss, semi-gloss (satin) and matt. Gloss is the most hard-wearing and matt the least. For a very durable surface with a matt or satin appearance, apply several coats of water-based varnish, follow with two coats of gloss and continue with matt varnish, sanding lightly between coats.

APPLYING VARNISH

Always varnish in as dust-free an atmosphere as possible. It is preferable to varnish in daylight and, if possible, with light from a window to reflect on the varnished surface, which will help you see whether you have completely covered it. A cotton shirt or sweatshirt is the best clothing to wear; wool can be a great hazard when varnishing as the fibres always seem to find their way onto the sticky surface. And above all do not let any pets near the wet varnish!

Use a clean brush with no loose hairs or dried varnish in it that might come off on your newly varnished surface. It is best to use quite new varnish. Try to buy the oil-based variety in particular in small quantities as it tends to thicken and 'yellow' in the tin over time. If you have to use old varnish, dilute it with a little white spirit, stir it well and strain the right amount through a nylon stocking into a clean jar. Stir the varnish gently, but thoroughly; never shake it as that causes bubbles. With matt or satin varnish, the additives that make them less shiny sink to the bottom so they should be properly mixed before use, otherwise the varnish will look glossy.

Dip your brush into the varnish one-third to half the way up the bristles, apply this to the middle of a small area and, using both sides of the brush in a flip-flop movement, apply the varnish spreading it out as far as possible in all directions. Then, with one side of the brush at a low angle to the surface, stroke the bristles lightly in one direction. Repeat from the centre of the next section, stretching the varnish back to meet the first and stroking back into it. Check that the whole surface is covered, if you have missed a bit go back over it only if the varnish is still quite wet, not if it has already started drying. If the varnish has started to dry make sure that you cover it properly with the next coat. Always check for runs (*see glossary*) once you have finished a coat before you clean your brush, so that you can disperse them with the tips of the bristles. Apply each coat in a different direction to the last.

LAYERING VARNISH

The idea of sanding the varnish between coats is firstly, to make each subsequent coat of varnish adhere and secondly to gradually reduce its thickness over the paper designs, but increase it over the background until the paper-ridge is finally obliterated, giving a completely smooth surface with the design appearing like inlay below the varnish. If you begin sanding after too few coats the design will be damaged. It is far better to build up a protective layer of six–ten coats of water-based varnish, which adheres to itself without

FAR LEFT. *This white decoupaged box has been given one coat of water-based varnish, followed by a mixture of five parts sanding sealer to one part shellac to age the prints slightly, then the box was crackle varnished and Raw Umber oil-paint rubbed into the cracks. The edges of the paper are still visible because very few coats of varnish have been given so far.*

LEFT. *The same box has now been given several coats of oil-based varnish, followed by three coats of 3-hour gold size which gives it its deep honey-coloured sheen. Water-based varnish cannot be used on top of the water-soluble top coat needed for the crackle varnish. The edges of the prints are now almost obscured and the decoupage is beginning to look like inlay.*

sanding in between coats, and dries in about half an hour, making it possible to get several coats on in a day. Then commence the oil-based varnishing, each coat will take between 12 and 24 hours to dry so can take some time. After the first two coats start sanding lightly between each one, with fine sandpaper or dampened Wet and Dry paper. Do not press too hard, just enough to 'key' the surface and remove the top skin over the paper cut-outs. Always wipe the surface with a Tak-rag (*see glossary*) after each sanding to remove the dust before applying the next coat.

The number of oil-based coats you apply depends mainly on how hard-wearing the item has to be or how smooth you want the end result. If you want a heatproof and scratchproof surface, as many coats as possible are needed, the exact number depending on the thickness of the paper and the varnish. It is better to have more coats of thin varnish than fewer coats of thick varnish.

Oil-based varnishes can take up to two weeks to dry thoroughly, even though they may appear dry on the surface. Items coated with it can be used during this time, but they will not have reached their maximum durability. And the more coats you apply the longer the drying process will be.

If I want a deep honey-coloured gloss finish, I sometimes use 3-hour gold size for the final one or two coats, instead of normal varnish. This is quite thick and very slow-drying so tends to level itself out leaving virtually no brush-marks. This is also used to stick the leaf in oil-gilding and for the first coat in crackle varnish, so if you have crackled a project do not use 3-hour gold size straight over it as you could end up with a crackle sandwich! Instead apply one or more coats of normal oil-based varnish first.

WAXING

Once your decoupaged piece has enough coats of varnish, you may wish to polish it with wax to give it a warm glow. Lightly 'key' the surface with 0000 wire wool and apply wax polish. This can be any furniture wax, or if you wish to age the piece, a stained wax. Various wood shades are available, all of which give an antique-look patina. Apply the wax with a soft cloth, massaging it into the surface. Leave to dry then polish briskly.

TINTING A VARNISH OR WAX

Oil-based varnish can be tinted with oil tube paint, so if you want to alter the colour of your project very slightly, blend a little oil-paint with some white spirit until it reaches the same consistency as the varnish and mix. By mixing purple into oil-based varnish you can counteract its yellowing effect.

To colour soft white wax, mix a small amount of oil tube paint directly into it.

PART TWO

PROJECTS

This section takes you on a tour of the house, showing a range of ways in which decoupage can give a fresh look to each and every room. Eight easy to follow step-by-step projects demonstrate how you can use the hand-painted sheets included in this kit to decoupage furnishings. In addition, each room features a number of inspirational decoupaged items illustrating many of the techniques introduced in Part One. All the methods are clearly explained or cross-referenced, and with the aid of a few basic materials you will be able to create original pieces you will be proud to display.

The HALL

The hall, be it large or small, is usually the first room guests encounter when they enter your home. It sets the tone for their visit and establishes the atmosphere of the house. It is also the initial dumping ground for shopping, outdoor clothes, visitors' luggage and wet umbrellas, as well as being the place through which people have to pass to reach the rest of the house. So, a very important and a well-used room that could easily become untidy, unless suitable receptacles for the 'debris' are placed there, such as an umbrella stand and various boxes like the ones shown opposite.

The large mirror in this hall is set facing the front door, giving extra light through its reflection. From the hall, doors open onto the sitting room and the kitchen and the stairs lead up to the first floor from it. In order to harmonize with the two rooms and the stairway and to create a bright welcome, the walls are painted in a pale shade, warmed by the rich brown of polished wood furniture and picture frames. Because of the simplicity of the colour scheme, we can add a multi-coloured flight of fancy in the shape of overblown roses, grapes, leaves and butterflies, which decorate the umbrella stand, hat box and watering can. The effect is that the abundance of the garden is brought into the hall to greet us, even in the depths of winter.

A FLORAL WATERING CAN

Decorating three-dimensional items has always fascinated me. Adorning useful objects is much more satisfying than merely creating flat pictures which are hung on a wall. I find that adapting a design to fit the different facets is a constantly pleasurable challenge. Decoupaging this watering can was no exception.

Many things used in and around the home are often ignored as items to be beautified because of their familiarity: enamel bread- or flour-bins, ewers, old fish-kettles, buckets, wooden spoons, flower pots and watering cans. If you think about it a watering can is an extremely pleasing shape! Well-balanced, with its practical cylinder for the water set off by the elegant spout and the moon-shaped top, each section requiring a different approach. In this project the body has been treated first. The main consideration being to make sure that there was enough space between the flowers and the border to avoid

a feeling of density in the final effect. The top was approached next. Aiming for asymmetry to refresh the eye, a group of auriculas was arranged on the left with fine branches draped to the right echoing the curve they follow. Lastly, the spout was decoupaged. Because its rounded surface is narrow in diameter, quite small flowers had to be used; so again, auriculas, cut singly this time, spiral up to the top. The insects were positioned last of all to find the most striking places for them in the overall design.

It has always been fashionable to paint tin and metalwork black, and before the advent of 'one-coat' or rustproof metal paints a primer was always used to protect the metal. The Red Oxide primer often used to paint metal is a beautiful colour in its own right and I came to the conclusion that it would blend, rather than contrast, with the subtle colours of the flowers selected for this project, forming an ideal background colour.

WHAT YOU WILL NEED
A galvanized watering can, old or new. Red Oxide oil-based metal primer, or car spray paint, or a 'one-coat' (rustproof) metal paint. Paintbrushes. White spirit or cellulose thinners to clean brushes (depending on paint used). One or two sheets of flowery wrapping paper. Gold wrapping paper. Decoupage scissors. Craft knife (optional). Water-based varnish. Strong oil-based poly-urethane, or gloss varnish, or 3-hour gold size.

1 Clean the can if necessary and paint or spray it with one or two coats of Red Oxide metal primer, or equivalent. Cut out individual and small groups of flowers, plus some extra leaves. Arrange them attractively with Blu-Tack, underlapping the central flower on each side.

2 Cut thin strips from gold wrapping paper with a craft knife, sticking these to top and bottom of the can before you stick the main design. Starting with undermost, stick all the leaves and flowers. For larger flowers, stick in stages (see step 1, page 77) to avoid wrinkles.

3 Dry overnight. Seal entire can with water-based varnish, checking first that all the edges of the design are firmly stuck. Let the varnish dry, then finish with a hard-wearing gloss varnish using a large brush for the cylinder and a smaller one for the more intricate areas.

4 Choose your varnish according to the type of finish you require and continue to apply additional coats depending on the level of durability needed. Is the can going to be subject to a beating of wind and rain, or just a splash of water whilst you are filling it up?

LEFT. *Two more decorative watering cans blend here with the one created on the previous page, demonstrating how practical objects can also be ornamental. A 'one-coat' metal paint was used as a base for both of these cans; the cream one had been in my garden for years! The design used on this can is the same as that used for the clock-face on page 79, showing its adaptability. The can was then crackled using Raw Umber oil tube paint (see pages 37–8) and then sealed with several coats of oil-based varnish. The green can was transformed from an old, chipped, white enamel one. The bright design used here contrasts effectively with the dark green background chosen.*

LEFT: *White china planters, such as the one on the right, are easy to find and inexpensive to buy. This one has spiral mouldings, which have been accentuated by adding alternate designs which echo the pattern. Baroque borders (see source-book list, page 126) have been washed with green paint and teamed up with the leaf border used on the clock-face design (see page 76). All are stuck with PVA glue and sealed, first with water-based, and then with oil-based, varnish.*

The enamel jug featured here is perfect for watering indoor plants; it has been given a coat of magnolia 'one-coat' metal paint and decoupaged with a beautiful Redouté rose. The print was sealed with water-based varnish before cutting because of the delicate nature of the stalk (see page 17).

BELOW. *A small tray is an ideal holder for keys and other items abandoned in the hall. The background of the print used for this tray (see page 124) was painted with two coats of black acrylic tube paint mixed with water to match its black emulsion base coat to avoid intricate cutting. A very small* brush *was required to paint in the fine lines. One coat of water-based varnish was then applied, followed by one coat of shellac. Two coats of crackle varnish were added, rubbing Payne's Grey oil tube paint into the cracks. The tray was finished with several coats of satin oil-based varnish.*

RIGHT. *A miniature hand-painted chest of drawers has been rejuvenated by adding strips and diamonds of marbled paper, mitring the strips at the corners (see page 29). It will need many coats of varnish – 15–20 ideally – before it resembles inlay. After the first ten, sand lightly between coats and wipe with a Tak-rag (see glossary). After two weeks, use wax polish to give it a soft patina.*

The papier mâché hat box was already painted mottled brown. Two loops of the swags that decorate the box were cut as one piece and the central areas painted with Raw Umber acrylic tube paint, dabbed on to match the mottled background, once they were stuck in place. The box was sealed with shellac and followed by several coats of satin water-based varnish. (See page 122 for motifs).

RIGHT. *This Victorian tin hat box was decoupaged directly over its original paintwork. The flowers were stuck in a band encircling the box and a line painted above and below, first with white acrylic tube paint and then, when dry, with a thinner coat of Venetian Red. After a coat of shellac, the box was crackle varnished, rubbing Raw Umber oil-paint into the cracks (see pages 37–8). Several weeks later the cracks had deepened and multiplied – perhaps the original paint had reacted with the crackle varnish – extra coats of oil-based varnish were needed to stabilize them.*

Toning strips of marbled paper, mitred at the corners (see page 29), were used on the maple frames. Matching butterflies have been stuck on each corner and the frame sealed with white polish for a glossy finish.

RIGHT. *This old cylindrical tin, bought from a jumble sale, made a wonderful umbrella stand when given two coats of black metal paint as a base. Large sections of wrapping paper, carefully cut for accuracy, were stuck in stages, as for the clock-dial (see page 77), from the centre outwards, taking care not to distort the stalks, and were smoothed with a paper towel to remove any air bubbles or wrinkles. The stand was given two coats of water-based varnish, crackled (see pages 37–8) and finished with two coats of oil-based varnish. Here, Raw Umber was rubbed into the cracks to make them show over the cut-outs; a paler colour could be used if you wished to accentuate the cracks over the black background instead.*

The SITTING ROOM

*T*he sitting room is a place for peaceful relaxation. In this room an air of tranquillity is created by soft, muted colours and the warmth of polished wood and old rugs. The creams and corals of the fabrics are particularly inviting and are enhanced by the contrasting turquoise in the tapestry cushions. All the shades of colour in this room are equal in tone; with no loud colours to startle the eyes, the result is a very soothing atmosphere.

This is a gentle room in which to talk, read, listen to music, stitch a tapestry or cut out scraps for a decoupage project. Anything too bright would be inharmonious, so the decoupaged objects featured here are subtle, both in colour and design. The patterns chosen verge towards the more traditional tastes of the eighteenth century, using black and white prints, hand-painted to echo the colours already in the room: the beige design used to decoupage the wine table blends comfortably with the colour of the sofa, for example. The lamp and photograph frame, situated on a side table towards the back of the room, have been decorated with a turquoise ribbon design, picking out the blue of the tapestry cushions and avoiding the possibility of monotony.

A GRISAILLE WINE TABLE

Having a great love of warm neutral colours and the grisaille painting often found in stately homes, I chose to combine the two in this decoupage design. This original, hand-painted composition of designs, included in your *Decoupage Kit*, was inspired by the grisaille tradition which imitates carved stone in both colour and texture. It is based on a classical motif of sheet music, lyre and trumpet, together with olive leaves. Often, the simpler the design, the more effective it is, so the border is a plain rope with rounded segments which are easy to bend around a curve (*see page 29*).

The neutral colour of this decoupage sheet was selected to match any background or colour scheme, making it an extremely versatile source material. This monochrome design can, however, be printed in any colour or shade you choose, with the help of a colour photocopier. To achieve this you print in a 'colour mode', green for instance, and by adjusting the colour balance buttons you can print in anything from emerald (by increasing the blue and reducing the yellow) to lime green at the opposite extreme. The design can also be printed in negative, giving any colour on a black background by adjusting the colour mode.

The success of any decoupaged item is largely dependent on the decouper's eye for colour and the balance achieved between the design and the space around it: the amount of space left is as important as the design itself. Too little space and the project becomes cluttered, too much and the design becomes lost or insignificant. Whatever the object to be decorated, its 'bone structure' is of vital importance. If the shape is downright ugly to begin with, no amount of artistic skill will turn it into a thing of real beauty! Always search for items with an endearing shape; it matters not how old or dirty they are, or even if they are slightly broken, the mends will not show once they are painted.

WHAT YOU WILL NEED
Small wooden tripod table. Medium and fine sandpaper. Paintbrushes. Lining brush. Acrylic primer/undercoat. Raw Umber emulsion or acrylic tube paint. Water. Methylated spirits. Paper towels. One sheet of decoupage design at A4 size and one sheet enlarged to A3. Decoupage scissors. PVA glue. Ultramarine acrylic tube paint (optional). Water-based varnish. Oil-based varnish. Wax (optional).

1 Sand the table with a medium-grade sandpaper until most of the shine is removed, to 'key' the surface. Then paint on three coats of acrylic primer/undercoat brushing with grain. Leave each coat to dry before applying the next.

2 Paint Raw Umber emulsion or acrylic tube paint, diluted with five parts water, sparingly over the white surface, again 'with the grain'. Allow to dry. Moisten a paper towel with meths and rub off the surplus brown paint to reveal the brush-strokes (see page 23).

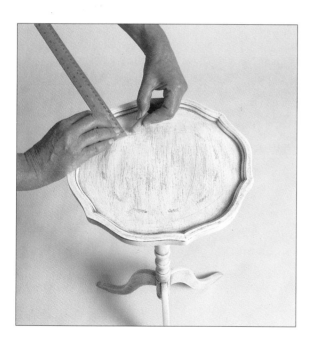

3 Using a ruler, measure 45 mm (1¾ in) in from the apex of each curve and from each angle on the table top and mark the points with chalk or pencil. Then join the dots to make a circle, which will act as a guide for the position of the leaf border.

4 Snipping between each leaf and the stem, ease the leaves into a circular shape (see page 29), fixing them in place with Blu-Tack. Stick the enlarged rope design to the outside edge of the table top and place the musical motif in the centre.

RIGHT. *As you can see the wine table blends beautifully with its setting. For a more dramatic effect, the same design would look wonderful on a black or dark green background. Alternatively, the design could have been printed in black and white for a stunning look on any coloured background. In a different setting, flower cut-outs, such as those used on the watering can (see pages 46–7), could have been used.*

5 *Mix a little of the diluted Raw Umber paint (used previously) with some acrylic primer/undercoat, to a pale brown colour to match the design. Using a short lining brush, paint a freehand line around the edge of the top and over the top of each leg (see pages 26–7).*

6 *Now stick down the cut-outs on the top of the table with PVA glue. Arrange and stick small sections of the A4-sized design to the sides of the legs. Then twine the rope design in a spiral down the central column of the table, and stick.*

7 *To tone down the brown shades, apply tinted varnish after a coat of water-based. Mix a small amount of ultramarine acrylic tube paint with water to a creamy consistency and add water-based varnish, testing it as you go until it looks just slightly blue when applied.*

8 *Paint with one or two coats of tinted varnish, then three or more of untinted water-based. Finish with two or more coats of oil-based varnish, matt or satin, sanding lightly with fine-grade sandpaper between coats. After two weeks, wax for a patinous finish.*

LEFT. *This coffee table has been given the same finish as the wine table by rubbing away the brown paint in places with meths. Then a border to match the cushions was added, using emulsion tinted with acrylic tube paint and mixed with water-based varnish to make it more transparent. Remember to draw the border on before you begin painting (see page 30). The design used on the wine table was also chosen for this project. For each corner a section of the oval leaf border (at A4 size) was cut in half and the top of each side exchanged to form a gentle 'S' shape. Because of the wear and tear this piece of furniture is likely to endure, the top must be sealed with several coats of oil-based varnish after the initial coats of water-based varnish.*

ABOVE. *Four of these wooden eggs have been gilded, and the fifth was painted with coral emulsion and decoupaged with cut-outs from a gold doily. The three gold eggs have been decoupaged with black and white prints washed and shaded with blue acrylic tube paint. The remaining egg has been decoupaged with marbled paper cut into small squares for a mosaic effect. For protection; at least eight coats of water-based varnish followed by two coats of oil-based are recommended.*

After two coats of white emulsion on the planter, black and white photocopied prints (see page 123) were stuck with PVA glue, then the whole surface painted with a mixture of one part shellac to four parts sanding sealer to soften the white. When dry, two coats of water-based varnish were applied. The inside was also painted and sealed with oil-based paint to make it waterproof.

LEFT. *In this selection of boxes the large one* (back left) *has magazine cut-outs of various boxes applied, overlapping from the back to the front with gold wrapping paper strips for the bevel around the top. The box* (front left) *was painted black and decoupaged with photo-copies of seventeenth-century lace designs* (see source-book list, page 126). *For the black box* (centre), *transfers were used* (see page 18). *The other three smaller boxes were all decoupaged with black and white photocopies, then sealed with shellac and crackle varnish* (see pages 37–8). *The dome-topped box has* The Birth of Venus *on top, with blue-washed, black and white photocopied prints for the sides. The octagonal black box* (front right), *started on page 30, looks effective with its jewellery cut from a magazine.*

LEFT. *Having painted the waste-paper bin with two coats of acrylic primer/undercoat, different chinoiserie prints were chosen, for the sides. The black and white copies of the prints were then sealed with sanding sealer and painted; first with thin washes of acrylic tube paint, in Yellow Ochre, Hooker's Green, Cerulean Blue and Venetian Red, then the shaded areas deepened with a stronger mixture of each colour. For the darkest areas a little Raw Umber was added to both the blue and the yellow. The surface of the bin was covered with PVA glue, slightly diluted to make the position of the print adjustable once applied. Then the cut-out was stuck down, and smoothed flat with a rubber roller. Finally it was sealed with several coats of oil-based varnish.*

RIGHT. *The old white china lamp (shown on page 24) was sponged and finished with blue bows and ribbons, cut from another of my hand-painted designs, to match this sitting room. The motifs were randomly positioned on the base to give an overall swirling effect. On the shade, the ribbon tails were stuck first encircling the bottom and the bows were placed at intervals afterwards; more space was left here than on the base to avoid a cluttered look. Both were coated with water-based varnish and the base finished with a coat of satin oil-based varnish.*

The photograph frame has the same 'meths-rubbed' finish as the tray on page 23. It was decorated again with sections of ribbon, joined together with individual roses from the clock-face design on page 79.

RIGHT. *This old mahogany work-box was bought over 20 years ago, so it was cleaned with white spirit and sealed with white polish before the designs were stuck. Copies of black and white prints were sealed with sanding sealer, then painted with a thin wash of Yellow Ochre acrylic tube paint diluted with water. The shaded areas were darkened with a mixture of yellow and Raw Umber, again diluted with water. When dry, the prints were cut out and stuck with PVA glue. Another coat of white polish was applied once the designs were firmly stuck and several coats of satin oil-based varnish were given to finish.*

The STUDY

A study needs to be reasonably well organized for dealing with paperwork, yet conducive to dreaming up new ideas. In this study there is a limited amount of storage space, so papers are stored away in practical box-files. The warmth of a cosy lamp and the company of a few 'old friends' like the ducks – their gilded surfaces adding a touch of splendour – provide the inspirational atmosphere. The colours, all important for tranquil creativity, include my favourites: turquoises and corals in the curtains and cushions, contrasting beautifully with the darkness of the oak panelling and polished mahogany. The antique, leather-bound books set the mood for some of the projects featured in the study; and the discovery of a wonderful Mexican rug contributed to the geometric design and glowing vivid colours of the box-file and lamp.

Box-files, an essential part of paper organization, need not be plain and boring. Why not decoupage them according to the subject of the information they hold? Here we have travel brochures in a box-file covered with an Ordnance Survey map and peppered on top with architectural drawings cut from magazines. The other one is decoupaged with tartan paper for teaching trips to Scotland.

A MEXICAN BOX-FILE

Usually inclined towards romantic curves, bunches of flowers and butterflies, in soft corals, greens and blues, I was determined, for one project in this kit at least, to find a dramatic contrast to that style and those colours! South America beckoned and books on old Middle Eastern rugs fell into my hands. I was searching for something with a fairly consistent, geometric pattern, like music with a regular beat, which would be easy to cut out, combined with the enticing deep colours of a Persian rug.

After much sketching I still had not found quite what I wanted. Then shopping in a local town one day, I passed a Mexican craft shop; the window was full of pottery in blues, greys and tans with brightly coloured, painted birds hanging from the ceiling. The temptation to enter was irresistible and on doing so a rug in wondrous colours immediately caught my eye. It had geometric diamonds and borders, each one featuring different combinations of the same colours, so no two were identical; another smaller rug boasted a plump geometric bird. The colours and shapes were just what I had been searching for.

The kind shopkeeper agreed to let me borrow the two rugs to use as reference. Little did I know, as I cheerfully carried them home, how long it would take me to get the balance of the design just right. Instead, armed with a sheet of squared paper, I began counting the squares as you would for tapestry.

This design could easily be adapted for embroidery or tapestry, perhaps using other visually stunning colour schemes. It would look wonderful in the browns and creams of natural wool, or the vivid colours of Peruvian knitting, for instance.

Because they are so geometric, the diamond motifs are extremely versatile. They can be used either horizontally or vertically, or alternately as a combination of the two. The variation in their size allows the design to fit any sized surface, start by positioning the larger motifs and filling in between them with the smaller.

WHAT YOU WILL NEED
A box-file (old or new). Shellac, or water-based varnish. One sheet (or roll) of green and one sheet (or roll) of red wrapping paper. One or two sheets of Mexican rug design (enlarged to A3). Large scissors; straight scissors; decoupage scissors. Liquid gum arabic. PVA glue. Paintbrushes. Craft knife. Paper towels.

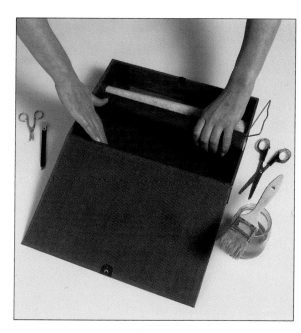

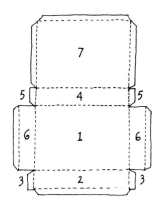

These two numbered diagrams show the order in which you stick the exterior and interior lining paper onto the box-file.

Exterior
1 bottom
2 front
3 side overlaps
4 back
5 side overlaps
6 right and left sides
7 top

1 Seal box-file, outside and in. Cut a piece of red paper large enough to cover exterior, allowing 5 cm (2 in) for overlaps all round. Paint bottom and front with liquid gum arabic. Place box on paper and stick flaps, smoothing into place with a paper towel. Stick down overlaps.

2 Cut two pieces of green paper for the interior sides, allowing a little extra at each end and at the bottom to overlap the corners and base of the box; stick with gum arabic. Cut and stick another piece of paper to cover the inside, leave edge of red overlap just showing.

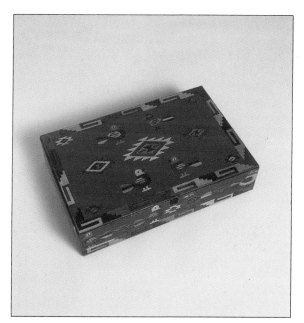

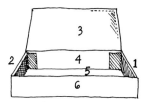

Interior
1 interior side
2 other interior side
3 inside top
4 inside back
5 inside bottom
6 inside front

3 Press lining into place with paper towel. Then cut out borders and motifs from rug design and arrange. Stick borders first with PVA glue, trying to make the colours match at the corners. Then stick the motifs, measuring with a ruler to ensure they are placed evenly.

4 Again, smooth all the motifs down with a paper towel so that there are no air bubbles trapped underneath them. When dry, check all are well stuck and seal with two or more coats of water-based varnish, depending on the finish you desire.

69

LEFT. *The cosy light given by this table-lamp suggested the use of the rug design immediately. Here it is set against a dark green emulsion background, which contrasts with the oak-panelling, and the turquoise used for the rings on the base and column accentuates that colour in the design. The diamond-shaped motifs have been up-ended this time. The larger ones stuck on the widest area of the base; the smaller ones up the column as it narrows and interspersed with the larger motifs on the shade. A circular template was used to position the motifs evenly (see page 31). To tone down the colours a coat of shellac was given, followed by a coat of 3-hour gold size to give a deep gloss finish. Acrylic spray varnish was used finally to seal the shade.*

LEFT. *Loving the fabric of these cushions and curtains, I was determined to use it for decoupage on a waste-bin. When decoupaging with fabric you must seal it first to avoid fraying when it is cut. To do this, hang the fabric up where the air can circulate around it and spray with fabric stiffener. Allow to dry following the instructions. Once the required motifs have been cut out they can be stuck with PVA glue. Here we added borders, using a lining brush and acrylic tube paint mixed to match the coral in the fabric. The bin was sealed finally with several coats of water-based varnish.*

RIGHT. *Two carved wooden ducks were gilded (see pages 32–5) and aged with Raw Umber acrylic paint. One was decorated with blue marbled paper using the template on page 101 and the other was 'mosaicked' with tiny squares of gold and marbled paper. To mosaic, cover about 5 sq cm (2 sq in) of the surface at a time with PVA glue and, using the tip of the glue brush to pick up the squares, place them on the sticky surface. Cover the area with waxed paper, press squares into place, carefully remove paper and repeat.*

The octagonal box was gilded (see pages 32–5) then decoupaged with clocks and watches cut from magazines. The box was then aged with a coat of shellac and sealed with water-based varnish.

Two more box-files were decorated in the same way as the one on page 69. The top one features an assortment of tartan wrapping papers and the other maps and buildings.

RIGHT. *The old wooden letter rack pictured here was given a new lease of life with borders cut from colourful marbled paper. The paper was folded and cut using a template to get a motif that was identical on both sides. The cut-outs remaining were then used on the ends. The letter rack was finished, when dry, with white polish.*

The box for playing cards was painted dark red, gilded (see pages 32–3), distressed (see page 34) and sealed with lacquer. To finish, hearts and capital As were cut from gold paper, stuck with PVA glue and the whole box coated with water-based varnish.

The small tray was sealed with shellac to give it a deeper base colour and black and white cut-out prints were positioned on liquid gum arabic. Two more coats of shellac were given when dry, followed by crackle varnish (see pages 37–9), with Burnt Umber oil-paint used in the cracks.

The KITCHEN

Whether it is large or small, the kitchen is one of the most important rooms in any home. Its importance stems not so much from the fact that our food is prepared and cooked there, but more from the fact that it is the heart of the home. This is the place where people gather frequently and informally to eat, to make a cup of coffee or grab a snack from the fridge and also to converse on the day's happenings, discuss ordeals or tell of triumphs, to seek advice or comfort, or merely to sit and relax. It is a room in which you unwind and unload all the experiences of the day, even in the literal sense! Therefore the kitchen has a tendency to reflect the various tastes, interests and occupations of the inhabitants.

In order to make it a comforting and comfortable room, this kitchen has been given warmth with a yellow water-based 'scumble' glaze on the walls. This immediately makes the room welcoming, even on the darkest day; the colour also blends well with the mellow shade of the old pine furniture. A kitchen table would not normally come to mind as an item to decoupage, but by giving it a cheerful border to match the chairs, a rustic homely look is created.

A COUNTRY CLOCK

A clock has the familiarity of an old friend as you frequently glance at it day-in-day-out to find the time. Why not make your own clock and by doing so add a touch of your personality to it? This clock was inspired partly by the design of one belonging to my grandparents, partly by early nineteenth-century Austro-German clock-faces from the Black Forest region and partly by the English porcelain designs of Newhall and Old Staffordshire.

The hand-painted sheet of roses, daisies and leaves used to decorate the clock was originally created to decoupage a watering can (*see page 48*), but with the small addition of a basket to hold the flowers for the arch, it was easily adapted to suit this clock. The arc of roses in the basket was cut from the oval of flowers, any section of which could be used with the addition of two or three extra leaves at each end stuck just underneath it.

The dial was photocopied from a hand-painted one and because it is quite large gives room for a horseshoe of flowers in the centre. It could be reduced in size to make room for larger designs at the corners and a border around the face if desired. Finally, to balance the whiteness of the dial a pair of leaves, cut from the border, has been stuck between each numeral.

The background of this clock is off-white, but the design would look wonderful over a stronger toning colour, such as terracotta, deep green or yellow, depending on the colour scheme it needs to match.

WHAT YOU WILL NEED
A clock-face shape: metal, plywood or MDF (like this one). Battery-operated movement and hands. Acrylic primer/under-coat. Emulsion (for top coat). PVA glue. One sheet of decoupage designs enlarged to A3. Number-dial (see List of Suppli-ers, page 126). Compass. Ruler. Pencil. Chalk. Decoupage scissors. Two paintbrushes (for emul-sion and glue). Water-based varnish. 'Crackle' varnish. Raw Umber oil-paint. White spirit. Paper towels. Oil-based varnish.

PREPARATION

Paint the clock-face with acrylic primer/undercoat. When dry, sand lightly with fine sandpaper. Apply a coat of emulsion in the colour of your choice and allow to dry. To make cut-out pieces adjustable, apply a coat of water-based varnish to dry emulsion. Using a compass, trace the centre of the dial and cut out (alternatively, it can be left whole, in which case paint the surface of the clock with liquid gum arabic to stick on dial). With a ruler, mark the centre of the top, bottom and each side of the painted face with chalk, joining the marks to form a cross. Using these marks, centre the dial on the clock-face and lightly mark four points with a pencil just under where the dial will go, to position it accurately before sticking.

1 Position dial equidistantly from each side using guide marks. Glue an inch section under the numerals XII and VI and stick both firmly. Lift up one of the loose arcs, apply 3–5 cm (1–2 in) of glue to each end and stick, easing outwards. Continue until both arcs are stuck.

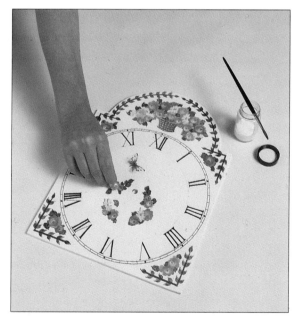

2 Stick borders first, snipping between leaves and curving them around arch. Arrange basket and flowers and stick in place. Leave ends unstuck and stick extra leaves underneath so they show when the clusters are glued down. Stick flowers, gluing from centre outwards.

3 Decoupage each corner. Then arrange some small flowers and leaves to form a horseshoe for the centre. Stick from either end, overlapping the flowers. Finish with a central motif at the bottom. Extra leaves should be stuck before the flower they are 'growing' from.

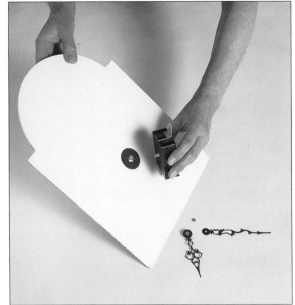

4 *When motifs are stuck, apply three coats of water-based varnish, then crackle varnish (see pages 37–9). Dry overnight and warm with a hairdryer until cracks appear; rub in Raw Umber oil-paint using a paper towel moistened with white spirit. Remove with clean paper towel.*

5 *Allow oil-paint to dry, then seal clock-face with oil-based varnish and dry overnight. To attach movement, place the tubular screw through the central hole, then attach hands to the shaft now protruding from the front, hour-hand first, and secure with small nut.*

RIGHT. Decoupaged with the coral roses provided in your kit, stuck on an ivory background and finally 'crackled' to give an aged look, this colour-ful clock will cheer up any morning. It is an ideal focus above a mantelpiece or in any kitchen.

6 *Should your crackles not be successful, remove the oil-paint (at step 4) with white spirit and the top coat of crackle varnish with water. Reapply the first coat of varnish and try the whole process again. For darker crackles, use Burnt Umber, or Payne's Grey oil-paint.*

RIGHT. *Glass bowls are versatile and very effective when combined with decoupage. For this bowl a shoal of brightly coloured fish were colour photocopied from a collection of old cigarette cards; some were duplicated at the original size and others enlarged, reversing them to get the mirror image. The fish were cut out as carefully as possible to retain their beautiful curves, which gives the impression of movement, and arranged on the underside of the bowl with Blu-Tack. They were then stuck with PVA glue and sealed with two coats of water-based varnish. Do not use oil-based varnish on glass as it tends to turn yellow with age.*

RIGHT. *Simple glass plates have been decoupaged on the underside with flowers and fruit and then painted green. The cut-outs were stuck straight onto the glass then sealed with water-based varnish. It is important to check that the edges are well sealed before painting over them to prevent the paint seeping underneath. Two coats of emulsion, enamel or oil-based paint should be applied, followed by two coats of oil-based varnish. The varnish should be left to harden for two weeks before immersing the plates in water.*

Buttercups and butterflies seemed appropriate to decorate this wooden, glass-lined butter-dish! The cut-outs were arranged asymmetrically over a cream emulsion base, then the box was crackled, rubbing Raw Umber paint into the cracks. The dish was finished using a matt oil-based varnish.

RIGHT. *These old pine chairs and the spoon-holder have all been decoupaged directly onto the wood, which was de-waxed first using white spirit and wire wool (see page 20) to ensure the glue would stick. Several coats of water-based varnish were applied to the decoupaged facets, then each piece was given two coats of matt oil-based varnish, followed by wax polish after 'curing' for two weeks.*

The tray has been decoupaged with the same design as the clock-face and the chairs. This time, however, the design was stretched into an oval shape when it was colour photocopied in order to follow the natural shape of the tray.

RIGHT. *This enamel bread-bin has been transformed since I found it chipped and decaying in a junk shop. First it was given two coats of rustproof metal paint, then a deeper shade of the same colour in water-based scumble glaze was dragged over (see page 21) to give a broken yellow back-ground, echoing the kitchen walls. The design was stuck, sealed with a coat of water-based var-nish, then finished with two coats of satin oil-based varnish.*

The same yellow scum-ble glaze has been used for the background on a matching tray, dragging it with the grain for a pleasing streaky effect. Straight borders were used, snipping between the different coloured seg-ments for the curved ends (see page 29).

The DINING ROOM

The dining room featured here is a spacious area on the first floor landing at the top of an open staircase. I felt it needed something to make it more intimate and cosy; the answer? a screen. Screens come in many different shapes and sizes, and have been synonymous with decoupage since their popularity in Victorian times when ladies of leisure passed their time decorating these large pieces of furniture. In those days, the fashion was to cover them almost completely in multi-coloured prints and scraps of paper. My approach, however, was to minimalize the decoupage for a more contemporary and stunning effect.

Since the area is fairly dark, and used as a dining room mainly at night, it called for a striking colour scheme, which would be enhanced by candlelight reflecting in the polished wood of the table. The curtains are covered in bright crimson apples which contrast with the emerald green of the leaves, so to make a feature of the screen, the green has been echoed. Green can be a cold colour, and too much would be a mistake, but here, silhouetted against the warm light shining from the hallway below, it gives the perfect partition, and forms an elegant backdrop for a happy meal with family or friends.

A Crested Screen

For this screen, I wanted to paint a design that was fairly simple and quite formal in style, so that it could be adapted for a variety of uses and to fit into almost any surroundings.

Browsing through a handbook of orna-ment one day, I came across some perforated crestings which caught my eye. They are carved wooden ornaments, which were used in the late nineteenth century to finish off the roofs of Swiss-cottage-style buildings, farm houses and pavilions. I thought this decoration would be an ideal theme for the

screen, so I developed the central motif for the design from the gable end of a roof. Its adaptation forms the top of the central motif, and is turned upside down for the bottom. Once that had been decided upon, it was a pleasing challenge to evolve matching corner-pieces. Designs have a way of taking over, and this one seems to have given itself a Gothic flavour. In addition, the larger, lozenge-shaped border (*see opposite page*), when cut into segments, can be interlaced to form an arch as on the wine coasters, giving a Celtic feeling. Both this and the segments of the smaller border can be snipped between to ease round any curve.

Once the borders had been designed, they needed something to join them. Two small motifs suggested themselves to me. The larg-er of the two has been used either side of the central motif on each panel of the screen and the smaller ones on the outside border. It was difficult to decide whether the larger motif should face inwards or outwards; finally I opted out of the decision and on the two outer panels it faces out, and on the middle panel, in! Even such a seemingly minor adjustment can make a difference to an over-all design.

Although the design has been painted in pale jade green to match the table-mats, it has been printed for this project in striking black and white and greatly enlarged to fit the scale of the screen. Alternatively it could be print-ed in any shade you like, using a colour photo-copier, to match your colour scheme.

The borders of this design would be ideal to use for frames or table-mats. The smaller ones could be used to form a trellis with sec-tions of the larger one placed in the dia-monds between. Four of the corner motifs would look wonderful at the corners of a table. I have used them on the black mat beneath the flowers just visible on page 88. The design itself is hopefully a useful one for the more masculine projects or presents.

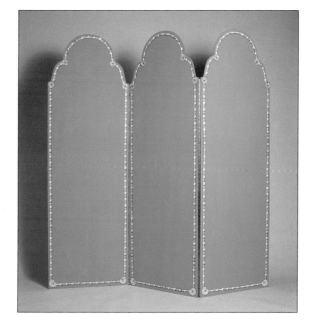

1 *First give the screen a coat of acrylic primer/undercoat, when dry paint with emerald green emulsion, a little brighter than the required end result. Paint on a section at a time in all directions, and then smooth with downward strokes before it dries.*

2 *When the emulsion is dry, attach the cut-out borders, printed in black and white, with Blu-Tack. Place at best distance from the edge. Keep the shaded areas of each border to the right and below. Position corner motifs in the appropriate places.*

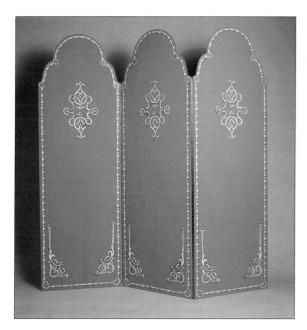

3 *Stick the borders with PVA glue, then cut out the background of the small corner motifs and stick. Then cut out the larger motifs and stick them in place with Blu-Tack, trying them at various heights until the best position is found. Stick with PVA glue when happy.*

4 *Carefully stick the large corners in place and when firmly stuck, coat with the one part shellac to five parts sanding sealer mixture. When dry paint with oil-based or poly-urethane varnish, adding as many coats as required to make the cut-outs look like inlay.*

LEFT. *The finished screen, placed in position at the top of the stairs, gives a charming background to this table for two, complementing the colour scheme and separating the area from the floor below.*

The candlesticks have been gilded with silver leaf (see page 33), then sealed with sanding sealer. Six segments from the larger border have been cut out and placed equidistantly around the thickest part of the candlestick, overlapping slightly. Four corner motifs have been applied to the cup and five small buds around the base, with five circular ones just above.

LEFT. *Stunning effects can be achieved with simple glass plates, making a beautiful platter on which to present a variety of food. To create this plate the decoupage design is stuck to the underside of the glass, using a template as a guide (see page 31), and sealed with water-based varnish. Then a border is painted around the rim to mask the uneven edge of the gilding. Next the underside should be gilded (see page 33) and finally sealed with two coats of oil-based paint and a coat of oil-based polyurethane varnish. Allow the varnish to harden for at least two weeks before hand-washing. The motifs used on this plate are reproduced on pages 122 and 123.*

RIGHT. *The borders of this table-mat were stuck first, mitring the corners (see page 29). Then the motif was positioned centrally and stuck in sections (see page 77). The paper bridges, which had been left for stability (see page 28), were cut off one by one and each delicate arm stuck from the centre outwards to avoid distortion and wrinkles. After six coats of water-based varnish, the mat was crackled (see pages 37–9) and finished with six or more coats of oil-based varnish for maximum durability.*

This octagonal bottle holder was sealed with shellac, painted with red-brown emulsion, gilded and distressed with wire wool (see page 34). Two segments of the larger border were placed interlacing on each facet, to form an arch, the smaller border was then stuck around the bevel.

RIGHT. *The reflected light from a mirror is ideal for brightening up dark corners. To avoid having to varnish on the mirror, the decoupage border was created on a sheet of plain glass which fits in front. The zigzag pattern was cut from gold wrapping paper using the template on page 124. Then strips of gold paper were cut and mitred to form an inner border. A coat of water-based varnish was painted over the decoupage as far as the middle of the inner border and two coats of black emulsion applied for the final dramatic effect. Both mirror and glass must be clean before sandwiching them together behind the frame. The glass plate below has also been finished with decoupage beneath the 'marbling' (see page 25).*

The BEDROOM

A bedroom must be a retreat, somewhere to escape to, away from the frenetic pace of daily life. It should be a peaceful haven by night, yet it must encourage our reawakening in the morning and fill us with the energy to face the challenge of a new day. Here, again, my favourite colours – coral, cream and turquoise – appear in the curtains, bedspread and cushions. I have attempted to enrich and enliven these colours with a refreshing pale green shade for the chest of drawers and the headboard.

My love of lace reveals itself in the choice of accessories for this room. It blends beautifully with the delicacy of the flowers featured in the design on the chest and headboard, which also incorporate the corals and creams, complemented by the soft green of the luxurious grapes. The clock-face and miniature chest of drawers are nostalgic in their use of old-fashioned black and white prints, reminiscent of eighteenth-century tastes; and the lace cloth and bedspread are echoed by the decoupaged tray and hand-mirror, utilizing paper doilies and simple white paper to achieve their 'lacy' effect.

PENNSYLVANIAN DUTCH DRAWERS

WHAT YOU WILL NEED
Chest of drawers (old or new). Medium- and coarse-grade sandpaper. Screwdriver. Pale green emulsion. Acrylic primer/undercoat or white acrylic tube paint. Raw Umber tube paint. Paintbrushes. Lining brush. Six or seven sheets of decoupage design (enlarged to A3). Scissors (straight and decoupage). Blu-Tack. PVA glue. Ruler. Blackboard chalk. Water-based varnish. Oil-based varnish.

The decoupage design for this project was originally painted with flexibility in mind. The motifs had to have a general appeal and be adaptable for use in groups, as wreaths or for borders. A collection of stylized flowers and fruit presented itself: something of the Pennsylvanian Dutch tradition, but also appealing to English tastes.

The phrase, 'Pennsylvanian Dutch', is derived from 'Pennsilvanian Deutch', giving us a clue to the roots of this style, which lie in what are now parts of Austria, Germany and Switzerland. Towards the end of the seventeenth century many people in those areas, having lost everything through local wars, were lured away by William Penn's promise of a new life in America. Memories of painted dower chests and wardrobes went with them and, once they had established their communities, the desire for traditional painting on furniture with the symbolism of old designs re-emerged.

The lily symbolized man's search for God and the promise of paradise and the urn was symbolic of the Holy Grail; roses did not emerge in Pennsylvanian Dutch until the nineteenth century. Traditionally daisies are not included, but I felt their shape complemented the design perfectly and their colours blend with and lighten the others. In addition, the three-dimensional nature of grapes has always fascinated me and their wonderful bloom is very appealing. Their green colour harmonizes superbly with the creams and corals of the flowers and I could not resist arranging some of them in an urn-like vase.

It is not essential to use all the elements of this design in one project. Grapes, daisies and the apricot-coloured flowers also look lovely alone; alternatively, try a combination of daisies and roses together with an abundance of leaves. The motifs from this sheet look attractive when arranged over any of the colours in the design. For the chest of drawers shown on the following pages I chose to pick out the colour of the grapes as the background shade. If more of a contrast is required these colours would also look stunning over yellow, black or brown, or even my beloved turquoise!

The headboard makes use of the urn of flowers from the decoupage design sheet again. This time, however, because the headboard is wider than it is tall, the extra flowers, grapes and leaves have been used on either side to follow the shape. Again the flowers were arranged with Blu-Tack initially and the undermost ones stuck first, ending with the central motif – the urn.

PREPARATION

Before you can think about arranging motifs on your chest, you must prepare the surface. As a chest of drawers is quite a large object you must set aside plenty of time for the initial stages. If you are decoupaging an old chest that is waxed, de-wax the surface (*see page 20*) before following the steps below. If it has an old coat of paint, use a medium-grade sandpaper to 'key' the surface, rubbing with the grain. Remove all loose paint and patch any chips with acrylic primer/undercoat, followed by a complete coat of acrylic primer/undercoat before painting on the green background colour. If the chest is brand new and you wish to retain natural wood as the background for your design, simply seal the sanded chest with sanding sealer, or shellac if a deeper shade is required.

1 Remove knobs from each drawer. Sand all the outer surfaces with medium-grade sandpaper, rubbing with the grain of the wood. Paint on one coat of green emulsion, brushing in all directions, then smooth the paint lightly in the direction of the grain before it dries.

2 When dry, using medium/coarse-grade sandpaper, 'distress' the paint at random intervals, always going with the grain. Logically, the paint would wear away at the edges and on the corners, with streaks and drifts of worn patches on the top, sides and drawers.

3 Next, using a lining brush, paint a line around the edge of the drawers, around the top and on the sides of the chest (see pages 26–7). Mix a little Raw Umber with white acrylic tube paint, or primer/undercoat, to a creamy consistency for the colour used here.

4 Cut out individual flowers and leaves and arrange them on the drawer fronts with Blu-Tack, facing outwards from the centre and overlapping each one slightly, until you are happy with the effect. Try to vary the pattern on each drawer, for balanced asymmetry.

5 For the sides, cut a complete urn of flowers, some extra leaves, flowers and grapes. Position the urn with Blu-Tack just below the centre, and add flowers and leaves above underlapping it, gradually increasing the height and narrowing towards the top.

RIGHT. *The warm corals in the design used on the chest of drawers have been picked out by a matching lampshade. The small wooden photograph frame, decoupaged with sandpaper, is simple but effective. Sealing the frame first with shellac, the corner designs, cut from medium-grade sandpaper, were stuck with PVA glue. Then the frame was given three coats of acrylic primer/undercoat, plus a coat of pale green diluted emulsion; when dry this was rubbed with methylated spirits (see page 23) to give a distressed look. Here I wanted to keep the ridge and texture of the sandpaper, so only one or two coats of water-based varnish were necessary.*

6 Stick all the designs, starting with the outermost leaves underlapping the flowers. Measure and draw the outside edges of the border for the top with chalk or pencil. Cut and arrange the design, again overlapping the motifs. Stick when happy with the final effect.

7 When the glue has dried, check all motifs are firmly stuck. Then seal with water-based varnish, adding more coats if you wish to conceal the paper edges. Then finish with two coats of oil-based polyurethane varnish, or more for a smoother or glossier surface.

LEFT. *As the clock-face decoupaged here was a brand new metal one it was painted white with a 'one-coat', cellulose-based metal paint. In this case the dial was hand-painted, but a paper one could be used just as easily (see page 77). Blue emulsion was used for the arch and the corners and, using a lining brush, the fine black lines around the edges were added (see pages 26–7). This was followed with a gilded line, achieved by laying small strips of Dutch metal leaf on a fine line of water-based size. Then the intricately cut prints were stuck, each of the corner pieces a combination of small motifs put together. When dry, the clock-face was sealed with white polish and then crackle varnished (see pages 37–9), finishing with two coats of oil-based varnish.*

LEFT. *The miniature chest of drawers has been stained rather than painted (see page 20). Borders were added to each drawer, the sides and the top, mitring them at the corners (see page 29). Marking the position of the handles for each drawer (slightly more than half-way up), the decoupage design was centred on each section.*

To make the little trinket box, it was first sealed with shellac and then blue emulsion borders painted on the lid and sides. Baroque designs were chosen and another coat of shellac added when dry. This item was crackled in the oven (an alternative method of drying the varnish) which was a little too hot resulting in the crackles lifting and peeling off. Antiquing this gave a different, but not unpleasant, effect.

LEFT. *Simple white paper doily cut-outs have given this sponged tray (begun on page 21) a lacy look. Because the paper is quite thin, the whole of the tray was painted sparingly with liquid gum arabic and the doily pieces smoothed into place while the adhesive was still wet.*

The old wooden hand-mirror has been given a new look by cutting out the template (see right) from white paper. The paper should be folded in half and half of the template traced onto it. Liquid gum arabic was used again for mobility and the design stuck from the centre outwards. A coat of shellac gave the white paper its aged look and satin oil-based varnish its sheen.

RIGHT. *Templates such as this one present infinite possibilities for decoupage if you just let your imagination roam a little. I tried to reproduce a lacy design for the back of the mirror, but the same template could be used in many different ways; with or without its border and on varying types of paper: marbled, coloured, gold or* silver. *Four of these shapes placed together to form a cross would make an ideal table-centre and two, end to end, a drawer-front.*

FAR RIGHT. *These patterns are the ones used for the miniature chest on page 99: you can enlarge or reduce them on a photo-copier for use on an original decoupage project.*

The BATHROOM

This small bathroom has been made stunningly sunny and cheerful with bold yellow and white striped wallpaper, which gives a spacious feeling. It is complemented by the deep blues of Chinese porcelain and blue and white striped towels. Continuing this colour theme and building on the glamorous character of the gilded mirror-frame, exotic additions have been made to match the overall scheme, making this bathroom a luxurious room to be enjoyed for more than just the quality of the plumbing!

The mirror conjures up the elegance and splendour of the early nineteenth century and so does the gilded tray with its fantasy figure on horseback. The glass bowl features the blue and white design sheet included in this kit, which was inspired by an old majolica plate. This type of earthenware, made in Italy since the thirteenth century, is glazed with brightly coloured metallic oxides giving it a rich glow, which I endeavoured to imitate here. More practical items, such as the glass jar, blue tooth-mug and containers for all those bathroom essentials continue the blue and white theme.

The attractively shaped corner-shelves enlarge the room and add interest, their triangular shape relieving the squareness of the mirror and the window, and providing the storage space for all those essential bits and pieces we need in the bathroom.

A GILDED GLASS BOWL

The most arduous element of decoupage is the final task of varnishing. If you are a perfectionist, the prospect of the seemingly endless coats of varnish required to render the surface as smooth as glass could deter even an eager decouper. In addition, the potential hazards that accompany each fresh coat of varnish – dust, strands of wool or fibres from clothing, hairs from a passing pet – can be frustrating in the extreme! A completely 'dust-free' environment in which to work is impossible for most of us to achieve, so minimum varnishing is certainly preferable. What could be better then, than to utilize real glass as the protective top surface? Impervious to all damage except accidental breakage, much of today's glass is inexpensive and does not discolour when non-yellowing, water-based materials are used on it. Do make sure that the water-based varnish you choose is one that will adhere to glass, however.

Imagine the infinite possibilities that decoupage on glass presents: sets of plates or table-mats to match any colour scheme, vases, jars, bowls, even surrounds for mirrors *see page 91*) or mounts for

pictures like the black and gold ones of the Georgian era.

When decoupaging on glass it is most important to double-check that the edges of all the cut-outs are firmly stuck before adding subsequent coats of varnish, or even more importantly before adding paint; if this should seep between the glass and the paper cut-outs it would be a catastrophe.

Having always loved the brilliant blues and yellows of fifteenth- and sixteenth-century Italian pottery, I was greatly influenced by the photographs in a book on early majolica and faience earthenware when designing the motifs for the decoupage sheet used in this project. The background colour for many of those plates and bowls was a glowing yellow ochre; I replaced it here by the irresistible richness of gold Dutch metal leaf, but silver or copper leaf would be just as eye-catching, and any colour paint could be used as an effective alternative.

WHAT YOU WILL NEED
An open-rimmed glass bowl. Two sheets of blue and white swags and ribbons design (enlarged to A3). Scissors (straight and decoupage). Template. Chinagraph pencil. Blu-Tack. PVA glue. Different sized paintbrushes (for glue, varnish and paint). Water-based varnish. Water-based or oil-based gold size. Dutch metal transfer leaf. Soft hair-brush. Sanding sealer or shellac. Oil-based paint. Oil-based varnish.

1 *A template like this one can be made from paper or card, with any number of divisions, using a protractor and ruler. Here we are using ten sections of 36° each. You can then work out the arrangement of your motifs on the template before trying them on the glass.*

2 *If you need to mark guidelines use a Chinagraph pencil, otherwise just follow the lines on your template, visible through the bowl. Arrange the motifs with Blu-Tack on the underside of the glass and stick with PVA glue when you are happy with the design.*

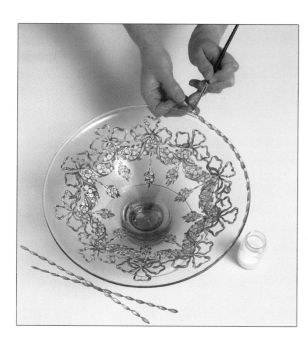

3 *A border of either paper or paint is needed to mask the edges of the Dutch metal leaf. Here the paper border matching the motifs was used. Curve the border (see page 29) and stick, painting glue on in sections. Finally, arrange and stick motif on base of bowl.*

4 *Seal the underside with water-based varnish. When this is dry, sparingly paint on a coat of gold size as far as the middle of the border; apply Dutch metal leaf while size is still tacky (see page 33), cutting sheets in wedge shapes and overlapping them slightly.*

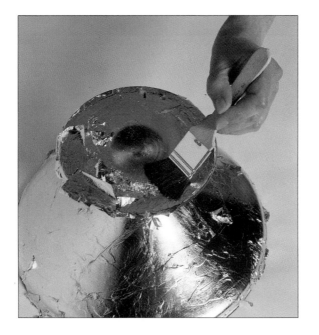

5 Having smoothed all the surplus leaf (not stuck to the bowl) into place, leave the gilding to dry overnight. Then remove all the loose bits of leaf with a soft-haired gilding brush (see page 33). Next, seal the metal leaf with sanding sealer or shellac.

6 When dry, apply a coat of oil-based paint, in black or a matching colour. Without it, gaps in the gilding are very noticeable, whereas with a coat of paint they can look deliberate. Allow to dry at least overnight, then apply two coats of strong oil-based varnish.

7 Allow the varnish to cure (see glossary) for at least two weeks before you attempt to immerse the bowl in water, to ensure that the seal is safe. Always remember to wash decoupaged items very carefully by hand.

RIGHT. *The finished glass bowl looks wonderful in this elegant bathroom. As an alternative the orange-yellow ochre of majolica plates, or the deep blue used over the leaf could have been used instead of gilding; even white eggshell paint would make an excellent background for the blue and white of the design. There are so many possibilities for motifs with which to decoupage a glass bowl such as this, for example, cut-outs of nuts and fruit, or simply strips of coloured paper spiralling up from the base.*

BELOW. *Two projects featuring the same design of blue roses are shown here. The round wooden box was initially given two coats of white acrylic primer/undercoat, the designs were stuck and two narrow paper borders added to the edge of the lid. The box was then sealed with water-based* varnish *and when dry, were crackle varnished, with Payne's Grey oil tube paint rubbed into the cracks.*

No initial preparation was necessary for the glass jar; the cut-out motifs were merely stuck to the outside with glue and followed with two coats of water-based varnish *applied sparingly and brushed downwards all round for an even finish. Oil-based varnish must not be used on glass as it has a tendency to discolour.*

The octagonal planter is decoupaged with a similar blue design, which has a more Chinese flavour.

RIGHT. *The butterfly tray on the middle shelf makes an ideal receptacle for soap, sponges and nailbrushes. After sealing and sanding the surface, it was given a coat of blue emulsion. When cutting out the butterflies their delicate antennae were removed and painted on* once the cut-outs had been stuck down. The border around the outer edge (visible on page 102) was curved by snipping between segments and easing into place (see page 29). For the inside border acrylic tube paint was applied using a short lining brush. The tray *was given a coat of shellac for an aged look and then two coats of crackle varnish for very fine cracks. Because of the dark background, white oil tube paint mixed with a little Raw Umber was rubbed into the cracks (see pages 37–9) and all was sealed with oil-based varnish.*

BELOW. *The designs used to decoupage the tray opposite are reproduced here for you to photocopy and use for your own decoupage projects. You will also need a reversed cartouche motif for this tray. All are featured in the copyright-free source-books listed on page 126.*

LEFT. *Before gilding (see pages 32–5), this wooden tray was sealed with shellac and painted with a terracotta emulsion in case cracks should occur in the leaf, which was laid on top. The black and white prints were enlarged to the scale of the tray, but before they were stuck the gilding was given a coat of shellac, and another was added once the prints were firmly stuck in place to age them. Finally, several coats of oil-based gloss varnish were applied to make it durable.*

The blue tooth-mug was decoupaged with bows and swags to match the gilded glass bowl. The swags were formed by curving the beaded border (see page 29) and were stuck directly onto the glass. Two coats of water-based varnish were applied sparingly, when the cut-outs were dry, brushing downwards.

111

The CHILDREN'S BEDROOM

*W*hen decorating children's rooms it is very tempting to use bright colours. Red is often chosen; however, it is a particularly stimulating colour that tends to prevent sleep, so it is not ideal when trying to get your little one to bed! In this room the vibrant colours are toned down by the tranquil blue shades that dominate the room.

Most of the designs featured here are easy enough to be carried out by a child. The toy-box and headboard designs are cut from sheets of coloured paper, using a series of basic templates (see pages 114 and 116) inspired by Pennsylvanian Dutch designs. These were simple, symmetrical shapes of flowers, hearts, birds and leaves, painted by the carpenters of immigrant communities from memories of the designs of their homeland. They had few tools to aid them, so most of the shapes were geometrically based, using only a compass and a straight edge.

For those children interested in stamp-collecting, it is so much more fun to stick them on to a pencil-box, which can be enjoyed daily, than merely collecting them in a book which is only opened occasionally! The lantern gives a child's room the perfect soft lighting for night-time, but remember to keep it out of reach of curious hands if it contains a naked flame.

A CHILD'S TOY-BOX

When I first started painting furniture in the early 1970s, long before decoupage had reclaimed its current popularity, it was as a result of reading an American book called *Peter Hunt's Workbook*. The author's style of painting was based on a single paint stroke, formed in the shape of a tear or comma. He then used various combinations of these brush-strokes to build up a design, whether a simple border or a more complicated pattern of birds and figures.

This book so intrigued me that I went straight to the library to research the folk art that had so obviously inspired him. Bringing home armfuls of books from Classical design to folk-art, I very quickly discovered that the common denominator was the very same tearshaped brush-stroke, whether on embroidery or pottery, painting or carving – from the Etruscans to Pennsylvanian Dutch – there it was!

Since then, many of my designs for painted furniture have been based on that same brush-stroke. Why not use the same tried and tested shape, cut from folded paper using a template, for decoupage? Most of us find one side of a symmetrical motif reasonably easy to draw, a heart shape for instance, but making the other side a mirror image is not so easy. By folding paper, drawing on one side and then cutting out the two layers, there are infinite possibilities, even for those who think they are less than artistic! The templates for the toy-box are very simple, inspired totally by the folk art and the often primitive style of Pennsylvanian Dutch artists.

WHAT YOU WILL NEED
Wooden toy-box (old or new). Sandpaper (various grades). White acrylic primer/undercoat. Pencil and ruler. Chalk. Blue and green emulsion. Water. Sponge. Paper towels. Turquoise, yellow, emerald and dark green paper. Templates of leaves, flowers and butterflies. Decoupage scissors. Blu-Tack. Paintbrushes. PVA glue. Water-based varnish. Oil-based varnish.

114

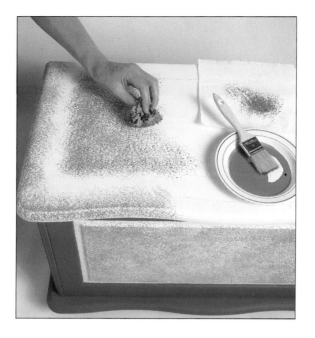

PREPARATION

If you are decoupaging a brand new varnished toy-box, remove most of the varnish by rubbing the box all over with medium-grade sandpaper. This ensures that the primer/undercoat will stick to the surface and prevent the paint from chipping off. If the box is old and waxed, de-wax it using paint-stripper, or wire wool and white spirit (*see page 20*). If the box has been painted previously, sand as before (*see page 95*). Paint on a coat of acrylic primer/undercoat, going with the grain. Then measure and draw the borders on the top and sides of the box, about 25 mm (1 in) in from the edge. Now paint a border over the white undercoat on the front with undiluted blue emulsion, leaving the top and sides of the box for now. (If the box you are using does not have a bevel around the front panel, measure and draw a border at this point.)

1 Dilute one part blue emulsion with four parts water and brush onto a damp sponge. Pat the sponge on a paper towel to remove the surplus paint and lightly sponge each panel (see page 21). Sponge the central area and the edges, overlapping the border.

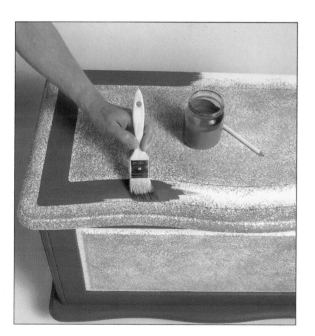

2 When the sponged areas are dry, reinstate the pencil lines for the borders and carefully paint them in with blue emulsion. Using a smaller brush, or lining brush, paint bevel, or line, around the front, top and end panels with green emulsion.

3 Plan design and cut motifs using templates on pages 114 and 116. When borders are completely dry, arrange cut-outs using Blu-Tack, so that they can be altered if you are not pleased with the overall effect. Mark the centre of each border first with chalk as a guide.

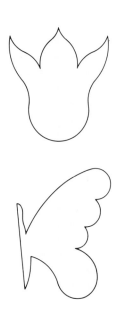

4 Stick the border design, with the leaves beneath the flowers, using PVA glue. Find the centre of each panel and mark the point with a cross, again using chalk. Now arrange the larger motifs with Blu-Tack, and stick when you are happy with the effect.

RIGHT. A similar arrangement of template motifs has been used for the central panel of this headboard as was used on the top of the matching toy-box. The shape of the headboard called for a simpler design, so the butterflies were not used in the corners. Apart from that variation the technique was exactly the same as for the toy-box.

5 Allow the glue to set overnight and check that all the edges of the cut-outs are well stuck. Next varnish the box with several coats of water-based varnish to conceal the paper edges, finishing with two coats of oil-based varnish for a smooth, durable finish.

LEFT. *This clock-face was prepared in the same way as the one on pages 76–77. Once the dial was stuck, the corners and the arch were painted green, then cream on top, leaving green borders, gilded lines were added to these applying the gold size with a lining brush. Victorian-style 'scraps' were cut into small sections and arranged around the centre, in the corners and on the arch. A coat of shellac was added to give an aged appearance, applied in circular sweeps to follow the dial.*

The red lamp uses the same style of motifs arranged randomly up the column.

For the paper parasol, pieces of coloured tissue-paper were cut in the shape of leaves and flowers. The colour of the larger flowers is achieved by sticking cut-outs in lavender blue and lime green together, to match the chest of drawers below. To decoupage this parasol, liquid gum arabic was applied to a section of it at a time and the motifs smoothed into place before it dried. No varnish is needed, but transparent lacquer can be used to seal the paper if required.

LEFT. *The chair and the chest of drawers were both distressed, but using different methods. The chest was distressed with sandpaper after being painted (see page 22). The chair, on the other hand, was distressed by streaking drifts of wax between a dark and a lighter coat of emulsion (see page 23). Panels were then painted on the chest in off-white, using a saucer as a guide for the curved corners. The edges of the panels were masked with strips of red craft paper. Both were then decoupaged with Victorian-style 'scraps' to continue the theme.*

The jigsaw puzzle was painted first with emulsion, then decoupaged with animals. Each piece of the jigsaw was given five coats of water-based varnish for durability.

119

BELOW. *This plain wooden box is easy enough for a child to do. It was first sealed with shellac, lightly sanded then, with the lid on, the stamps were stuck randomly all over it. Where the stamps cover the lid's join a craft knife was used to cut neatly through the small gap. All the edges were checked and re-stuck where necessary then sealed with water-based varnish.*

ABOVE. *The butterfly pictures are old cigarette cards stuck to mountboard. Strips of marbled paper, mitred at the corners (see page 29), form the surrounds and a fine waterproof pen was used to enclose the outer water-colour washlines.*

To continue the theme the white china lamp also features blue butterflies, randomly stuck and sealed with two coats of water-based varnish.

RIGHT. *A lantern is perfect for a warm glow with just a night-light inside. It is easy to get a stained glass effect by cutting out diamonds, triangles and strips of coloured gel film. Transparent lacquer was painted on to the glass, one pane at a time, and the pieces of gel applied while it was still wet. Two coats of water-based varnish were given to finish.*

GLOSSARY

acrylic primer/undercoat Matt water-based paint bound with acrylic, used for sealing or 'priming' surfaces, or as an undercoat. Can be mixed with any water-based emulsion.

acrylic tube paint Water-based tube paint which, when used in a thick consistency, can imitate oil-paint and, when used in a thin consistency, imitates watercolour. Waterproof when dry.

aniline dyes Powdered spirit dyes for mixing with methylated spirit, or any substance with a meths base. Highly toxic; wear rubber gloves and a mask during use.

Blu-Tack Putty-like substance, which will stick to any surface; does not harden so is ideal for temporary use.

burnish A rubbing action, either to make a surface smooth, or gilding bright.

casein Glue or paint binder, extracted from the whey of milk.

collage Layers of paper designs applied on top of each other or overlapping.

crackle varnish Cracked, transparent effect created by applying liquid gum arabic over nearly dried 3-hour gold size. The gold size contracts as it continues to dry, causing the cracks in the top coat.

cure Drying until completely hard. This is necessary for oil-based substances and can take up to two weeks, although the surface feels dry after two hours.

decalling fluid Fairly thick, milky, water-based liquid for making your own transfers from prints. The ink impregnates the fluid, which dries to plastic-like elastic film.

distemper Thick, water-based paint, traditionally used for painting ceilings and walls. Bound with casein or egg, making it softer and more absorbent than emulsion.

Dutch Metal leaf Imitation gold leaf made from copper and zinc.

emulsion Opaque, water-based wall paint, known as 'latex' in the US.

emulsion glaze Thin, milky, water-based liquid for making transparent, coloured glazes from water-based emulsions, acrylic tube paints or gouache.

Evostick Brand name of white, water-based glue, bound with polyvinyl acetate. Looks white and creamy when wet, but dries to transparent.

gel film Transparent coloured gelatine film, looks like thick cellophane; used over theatre lights to tint them.

gesso (pronounced jesso) Thick, creamy substance made from powdered chalk and rabbit-skin size. Several coats should be applied to a surface and sanded until totally smooth. Used mainly under gilding.

gold size Adhesive used for gilding; it is applied to a surface and the leaf stuck onto it. Available in water-based or oil-based size; the latter can also be used as a varnish, and as the first coat of 'crackle varnish'.

Gouache Water-based tube paint, water-soluble when dry, a little thicker and more opaque than watercolour or acrylic paint.

keying Roughening a smooth surface with sandpaper or Wet and Dry paper to help subsequent coats adhere. A coat of PVA glue can be used on glass or china.

knotting Methylated spirit- or alcohol-based liquid, used for sealing knots in new wood to prevent any sap escaping and damaging subsequent coats of paint.

liquid gum arabic Liquid gum or glue made from granules of dried sap from trees growing in Arabia. Can be used for sticking and for the top coat of 'crackle varnish'.

Low-tack tape Masking tape with a less sticky backing than normal masking tape, ideal for use over a painted surface as it is less likely to damage it.

MDF (Medium Density Fibreboard) Ultra-smooth board used in place of wood.

mountboard Thick card used to cut out surrounds or 'mounts' for pictures.

paper sizes For use in the step-by-step projects, the decorative sheets included in this kit have been colour photocopied at either A4 size (210 × 297 mm [$8\frac{1}{4}$ × $11\frac{3}{4}$ in]) or A3 size (297 × 420 mm [$11\frac{3}{4}$ × $16\frac{1}{2}$ in]). The sheets themselves are 210 × 259 mm ($8\frac{1}{4}$ × $10\frac{1}{8}$ in).

patina Gloss produced by age from polishing or handling a surface.

PVA glue Polyvinyl acetate glue. White when wet, transparent when dry; has a hard but plasticky feel.

Rabbit skin size Glue that comes in a dry, granular form; soak overnight in water and warm before use as binder for homemade paint.

rubber roller Can be used over decoupage cut-outs to ensure they stick.

runs Unsightly dribbles of paint or varnish, which occur when too much has been applied; difficult to remove when dry so try to avoid them (*see 'sparingly'*).

sanding sealer Methylated spirit- or alcohol-based liquid, fairly matt and almost colourless, normally used for sealing new wood prior to sanding it. Can be used to seal paper prints or, mixed with shellac to deepen the colour, for an antique effect over paint or decoupage.

scumble glaze Oil- or water-based glaze. Slow drying for a textured, transparent, coloured finish on top of paint. Tint oil-based glaze with oil tube paint and water-based glaze with acrylics or emulsion.

shellac Methylated spirit-based lacquer, treacle coloured, good for sealing bare wood and ageing prints or paintwork, giving a honey-coloured tint. Can be mixed with any other methylated spirit-based liquid or dye such as sanding sealer, white polish, transparent lacquer or aniline dyes.

size Normally used for sealing surfaces to make them non-absorbent. Can also refer to glue as in wallpaper size or gold size.

Smootherite Brand name for cellulose-based, rustproof paint for metal. Although glossy, it is compatible with water-based glues and varnishes, acrylic paints, oil-based or spirit-based products.

sparingly Dip paintbrush $\frac{1}{4}$ to $\frac{1}{3}$ of the way up the bristles and, using both sides of the brush in a flip-flop motion, spread the substance as far as possible in all directions as quickly as possible. Smooth over that section with the tips of the bristles in one direction and move on to the middle of the next section and repeat.

Spray Mount Adhesive that can be sprayed on to paper or card, allowing for repositioning. Long-term results for decoupage not known.

'tacky' The surface feels dry when lightly stroked with the fingers, and just sticky when firmly pressed with a knuckle.

Tak-rag Thin gauze, impregnated with mixture of oil-based varnish and linseed oil, used to remove fine particles left on painted or varnished surface after sanding, before next coat. Kept in plastic bag or sealed jar when not in use to keep moist.

Transparent lacquer Clear, methylated spirit-based lacquer, also known as French Enamel Varnish. Used as a sealer over gilding; can be mixed with shellac, sanding sealer, white polish and aniline dyes.

tube paint Artists' colours, available in oil, alkyd, acrylic, gouache or watercolour. Oil-based products can be tinted with oil or alkyd tube paints and water-based products with acrylic, gouache or watercolour.

Uni-bond Brand name of white, water-based glue, bound with polyvinyl acetate. Looks white and creamy when wet, but dries to transparent.

washlines Highly diluted watercolour borders and lines on mounts for pictures.

Wet and Dry paper Like sandpaper, but grey or black; made from chips of silicone carbide, a more resilient material than sandpaper. It is waterproof so can be used either with a dry or dampened surface for a better grip.

white polish Methylated spirit- or alcohol-based liquid, similar to French polish. It is not heat- or alcohol-proof, so can only be used over decoupage that will not be exposed to wear and tear. Can be followed with oil-based varnish to make it more durable. Can also be used to seal prints in place of sanding sealer, but gives a more brittle feel to the paper.

LIST OF SUPPLIERS

Mail-order available.

UNITED KINGDOM

*Belinda Ballantine, The Abbey Brewery, Malmesbury, Wiltshire SN16 9AS. Tel. (0666) 822047 Fax (0666) 822293
For all decoupage materials, including hand-painted designs featured in this book. Also numberdials featured on page 76.
Coln Galley, 19 West Market Place, Cirencester, Gloucestershire GL7 2AE. Tel. (0285) 659085
For all gilding and artists' materials, wrapping paper and coloured papers.
Constable Publishers, 3 The Lanchesters, 162 Fulham Palace Road, London W6 9ER. Tel. (081) 741 3663 Fax (081) 748 7562
For the full range of Dover decoupage source-book publications.
*L. Cornelissen & Son Ltd., 105 Great Russell Street, London WC1B 3RY. Tel. (071) 636 1045 Fax (071) 636 3655
For all gilding and artists' materials.
*The Dover Bookshop, 18 Earlham Street, London WC2H 9LN. Tel. (071) 836 2111 Fax (071) 836 1603
For decoupage print source-books.
General Trading Company Ltd., 144 Sloane Street, London SW1X 9BL. Tel. (071) 730 0411 Fax (071) 823 4624
For a selection of wrapping paper.
*Green and Stone of Chelsea, 259 Kings Road, London SW3 5EL. Tel. (071) 352 0837 Fax (071) 351 1098
For paints, paint finishes, specialist brushes, cut-outs, water-based scumble and varnishes.
*Hawkin & Co., Saint Margaret, Harleston, Norfolk IP20 0PJ. Tel. (0986) 82536 Fax (0986) 82228
For copies of Victorian 'scraps'.
Penny Kennedy Design Ltd., Unit 4, Lomond Industrial Estate, Alexandria, Dunbartonshire G83 0TL. Tel. (0389) 55516
For Tartan and Provençal wrapping paper.

London Graphic Centre, 107-115 Long Acre, London WC2E 9NT. Tel. (071) 240 0095 Fax (071) 831 1544
For Plaka (casein) paint, ceramic paints, coloured papers.
John Myland Ltd., 80 Norwood High Street, London SE27 9NW. Tel. (081) 670 9161/2 Fax (081) 761 5700
For shellac, sanding sealer, transparent lacquer, aniline dyes, Raw Umber emulsion, coloured waxes.
Panduro Hobby, Westway House, Transport Avenue, Brentford, Middlesex TW8 9HF. Tel. (081) 847 6161 Fax (081) 847 5073
For unfinished items to decoupage.
Paper & Paints Ltd., 4 Park Walk, London SW10 0AD. Tel (071) 352 8626 Fax (071) 352 1017
For paints, varnishes, paintbrushes, water-based scumble and varnish.
*E. Ploton (Sundries) Ltd., 273 Archway Road, London N6 5AA. Tel. (081) 348 0315 Fax (081) 348 3414
For all gilding and artists' materials.
Roberson & Co. Ltd., 1A Hercules Street, London N7 6AT. Tel. (071) 272 0568 Fax (071) 263 0212
For all artists' materials, including liquid gum arabic.
*Stuart R. Stevenson, 68 Clerkenwell Road, London EC1M 5QA. Tel. (071) 253 1693 Fax (071) 490 0451
For gilding materials and artists' colours.

UNITED STATES

Dover Publications Inc., 31 East 2nd Street, Mineola NY 11501. Tel. (516) 294 7000 Fax (516) 742 5049
For decoupage source-books.
The National Guild of Decoupers, 807 Rivard Boulevarde, Grosse Pointe, Michigan 48280. Tel. (313) 882 0682

CANADA

Folk Art Etc. Inc., 2621 Portage Avenue, Winnipeg MB R3J 0P7. Tel. (204) 888 0606 Fax (204) 888 0606
For folk art and decorative supplies and unfinished wooden items.
Ontario Crafts Council, Chalmers Building, 35 McCaul Street, Toronto ONT M5T 1V7. Tel. (416) 977 3551 Fax (416) 977 3552
For information about decoupage suppliers.
Woolfitt's Art Enterprises Inc., 390 Dupont Street, Toronto ONT M5R IV9. Tel. (416) 922 0933 Fax (416) 922 3017
For all art supplies and marbled papers.

AUSTRALIA

The Folk Art Studio, 178 Sydney Road, Fairlight 2094. Tel. and Fax (02) 949 7818
For all craft and decoupage materials, including paper and wooden items.
*Janet's Art Supplies and Art Books, 145 Victoria Avenue, Chatswood 2067, Sydney. Tel. (02) 417 8572 Fax (02) 417 7617
For decoupage kits and materials, papers, 'scraps', and unfinished wooden items.
*Oxford Art Supplies Pty Ltd., 221-223 Oxford Street, Darlinghurst 2010, Sydney. Tel. (02) 360 4066 Fax (02) 360 3461
For general art supplies.
Paper'N'Things, 88 Union Street, Malvern, Victoria 3144. Tel. (03) 576 0223
For all decoupage materials.

SOUTH AFRICA

Barney's Paint Centre, Fourways Shopping Centre, Bryanston, Johannesburg.
Wardkiss Homecare DIY Superstores, Cape Region, PO Box 30094, Tokai 7966. Tel. (021) 72 5000
Both supply liquid gum arabic, shellac products, 'Press-stick' (Blu-Tack), water-based varnishes and dutch metal leaf.

FURTHER READING

Davidson, Alex. *Interior Affairs*, London, Ward Lock, 1986
de Dampierre, Florence. *The Best of Painted Furniture*, London, Wiedenfeld & Nicholson, 1987
Hayden, Ruth. *Mrs Delany and her Flower Collages*, London, British Museum Press, 1992
Hodges, Felice. *Period Pastimes*, London, Wiedenfeld & Nicholson, 1989
Manning, Hiram. *Manning on Decoupage*, London, Constable, 1980
McCloud, Kevin. *Kevin McCloud's Decorating Book*, London, Dorling Kindersley, 1990
Moxley, Juliet. *Decoupage*, London, Charles Letts, 1992
Singleton, Nerida. *Decoupage: an illustrated guide*, Australia, Sally Milner Publishing, 1991

SOURCE-BOOKS
The following books and many more containing black-and-white prints are produced by Dover Publications, Inc., New York.
Cirker & Cirker. *Monograms and Alphabetic Devices*, 1970
Hasbrouck Rawlings, Eleanor (ed.). *1001 Scrolls, Ornaments and Borders*, 1979
Hasbrouck Rawlings, Eleanor (ed.). *The Cornucopia of Design and Illustration*, 1984
Hasbrouck Rawlings, Eleanor (ed.). *Decoupage: The big picture sourcebook*, 1975
Stella, Jaques (ed.). *Baroque Ornament and Design*, 1988
Vecellio, Cesare. *Pattern Book of Renaissance Lace*, 1988

INDEX

AUTHOR'S
ACKNOWLEDGEMENTS

My huge thanks to Eddison Sadd Editions for asking me to do this book and to Ian, Zoë, Elaine and Sarah for their immeasurable help and guidance in doing so; to Sue and Kirsty for the photographs and their patience and sense of humour; to Liz and Colin Legge, Paul von Fulman and the Malmesbury Preservation Trust for so generously allowing us to take over their beautiful houses for the location shots; to MFI Furniture Ltd. for kindly donating the chest of drawers, headboards and toy box; to Texas Homecare for the wine table; to Quetzal for the loan of their beautiful rug; to The Workbox, Malmesbury, for the rug in the Children's Bedroom; and to Penny Kennedy for her tartan paper. Most of all, my greatest thanks to Sally Richmond for her unfailing support and months of hard work in helping with all the decoupage projects, without whom it would not have been possible. So much thanks too to all the other willing helpers who have cut, stuck and varnished: Carolyn Lort Phillips, Kate Morley, Roz Coward, Helen Richmond, Ava Chance, my daughters, Antonia and Georgina Ballantine, and assistants Scot Dunn and Karla Jobbins.

EDDISON · SADD EDITIONS

Project Editor	Zoë Hughes
Proofreaders	Nikky Twyman
	and Marilyn Inglis
Indexer	Dorothy Frame
Art Director	Elaine Partington
Designer	Sarah Howerd
Production	Hazel Kirkman
	and Charles James

Eddison Sadd would like to thank National Gallery Publications for their kind permission to use their wrapping paper in the decoupage projects featured in this book.